Also By James Marsh Sternberg, MD

TRUMP SUIT HEADACHES

THE FINESSE; ONLY A LAST RESORT

BLOCKING AND UNBLOCKING

PLAYING TO TRICK ONE

With Danny Kleinman

SECOND HAND HIGH, THIRD HAND NOT SO HIGH

AN ENTRY, AN ENTRY, MY KINGDOM FOR AN ENTRY

L O L : LOSER – ON - LOSER

PLAYING
TO
TRICK ONE

There are No Mulligans In Bridge

JAMES MARSH STERNBERG MD (DR. J)

authorHOUSE

AuthorHouse™
1663 Liberty Drive
Bloomington, IN 47403
www.authorhouse.com
Phone: 833-262-8899

Published by AuthorHouse 10/18/2021

ISBN: 978-1-6655-0321-1 (sc)
ISBN: 978-1-6655-0320-4 (e)

Library of Congress Control Number: 2020919432

THIS BOOK IS DEDICATED TO

THE MEMORY OF

MARSHA MAY

STERNBERG

A WORLD CLASS WRITER

YOU WILL ALWAYS BE MISSED

BUT YOU WILL NEVER BE FORGOTTEN

CONTENTS

ACKNOWLEDGMENTS

This book would not have been possible without the help of several friends. Frank Stewart, Michael Lawrence, Anne Lund, and Eddie Kantar all kindly provided suggestions for material for the book.

I am forever indebted to Hall of Famer Fred Hamilton, the late Bernie Chazen, and Allan Cokin without whose guidance and teaching I could not have achieved whatever success I have had in bridge.

I want to thank my friend and editor, Danny Kleinman, a great writer, who contributed some ideas to this second edition and made many corrections. The remaining errors are mine.

And of course, I want to thank Vickie Lee Bader, whose love and patience helped guide me thru the many hours of this endeavor.

James Marsh Sternberg, MD

Palm Beach Gardens, FL

FOREWORD TO THE SECOND EDITION

Less than a year after its publication, Jim Sternberg has revised and expanded his book *Playing to Trick One*. Taking his own "Mulligan," Jim has amazed and delighted me with his zeal and energy in making improvements, large and small, upon the first edition.

In this new edition, Jim sprinkles his chapters with new interesting deals, explains auctions more fully, and adds some fresh perspectives.

Here also, the cards are spread out and easier to read, and a full table of contents lists and numbers all the deals. This facilitates partnership discussion, which I highly recommend, especially about defense.

For ease of understanding, Jim shows all four hands at the top of each page. But to get the most from each deal, try covering all the cards except yours and dummy's before deciding what to play to Trick 1. I had suggested concealing the two unseen hands until after the explanations, but that would make the play more difficult to follow.

In this book, refreshingly, the form of contest is rubber bridge or its sister at duplicate, IMPs. Many of the mistakes we make stem from playing most of our bridge at matchpoints, a form of contest that has its own merits.

But matchpoints also engenders bad habits. Because it is a timed contest, we sometimes play too quickly. In our zeal for tops, we often try for every trick that isn't tied down. The dual arts of safety plays, and desperate gambits that risk extra undertricks trying to make iffy contracts, suffer neglect. However, even at matchpoints they remain relevant in contracts that the "field" may not reach, a category that includes most slams.

Don't worry about overtricks or extra undertricks here. Focus on making or breaking contracts. Sit back, take your time, enjoy the many neat problems, and learn. I hope you'll need fewer "mulligans" when you play.

---Danny Kleinman

PRELUDE TO THE SECOND EDITION

Why a second edition so soon? Most often it's because the first edition has sold out. I wish that were the case here, but I'm sure if you look really hard, you can find a copy of the first edition. The truth is while I have written many articles for most well known bridge magazines, and some not so well known, "Playing To Trick One" was my first attempt at writing a book. And as you can see on a previous page, I've written quite a few more since.

But I also thought I could improve on the first edition. I have learned a lot from my editors, my co-author on a few, my publisher and others. Probably 95% of the deals are the same, but some new deals have been added, the lay-out of the cards is improved, and explanations of the bidding is better where before often there was none. I like the cover better, the deals are titled and are in a table of contents.

I hope no one writes and tells me I better get started on a third edition.

James Marsh Sternberg, MD

Palm Beach Gardens, FL

mmay001@aol.com

INTRODUCTION

Bridge is a game of mistakes. The best players make fewer mistakes. It's not a matter of being brilliant. The real expert players never make basic mistakes, they keep the ball in the court, in the fairway. Sure there is an occasional deal where they make a brilliant play but that's not what distinguishes the true expert from the good player.

Many say the opening lead is the most important play in bridge. That's certainly often true. But another top play is trick one. One of the biggest mistakes non-expert players make is playing to Trick One quickly, then looking around and deciding what to do next. And in many cases, it's already too late. The key to the hand was Trick One.

But sorry, no mulligans in bridge.

This book will present a series of deals, all as quizzes but of course you have a big clue from the title. We are always using IMP scoring. Only making or defeating the contract is important. Ignore extra over or undertricks that would matter at matchpoint scoring. I hope you will find the deals and following discussions interesting enough to help you learn to do your thinking before, not after you play that first card. Speed kills.

WHEN TO DUCK

To duck or not to duck, that is the question. Probably without seeing the deal, the answer is yes. But there are so many considerations; every deal has a slightly different twist. And there are no set rules; there are many different reasons for ducking.

So let's look at a series of deals and consider the question. And obviously, it's a Trick One decision.

DEAL 1. SUIT WELL STOPPED? MAYBE NOT

♠ A 3 2
♥ 7 2
♦ Q J 10 9 7
♣ K Q 4

♠ J 5
♥ K Q 8 6 5
♦ A 3 2
♣ 5 3 2

♠ Q 9 8 7
♥ 10 3
♦ K 6 5
♣ 9 8 7 6

♠ K 10 6 4
♥ A J 9 4
♦ 8 4
♣ A J 10

West	North	East	South
P	P	P	1♣
1♥	2♦	P	2NT
P	3NT	All Pass	

Opening Lead: ♥ 6

East played the heart ten, South the jack, thinking she had the suit "well stopped". She led a diamond, East won and returned his last heart. Sure, now South ducked.

West won the eight and continued the king. West got in with the diamond ace to cash two more heart tricks, down one.

Was the heart suit "well stopped"? Could South have prevailed?

Sure, just duck the first trick to break later communication between the defender's hands. Play the jack at Trick 2 which loses but when East gets in, he has no hearts. It's unlikely West has both the AK of diamonds as a passed hand.

Bridge players sometimes ask, "Which should I count, winners or losers?" It's best to count both. Winning the ♥J gives you ten winners but leaves you with five losers. The trouble is the defenders can get their five before you can get your ten. Ducking costs a meaningless tenth winner but saves you a crushing fifth loser. It's a race you want to win.

DEAL 2. ANOTHER NINE BEFORE FIVE

```
                  ♠ A 7 3
                  ♥ K Q
                  ♦ Q J 10 9 8 5
                  ♣ J 8

   ♠ K 5                        ♠ J 10 9 8 4
   ♥ 10 9 7 6 3 2               ♥ 8 5
   ♦ K 3                        ♦ A 6
   ♣ 6 5 4                      ♣ K Q 9 2

                  ♠ Q 6 2
                  ♥ A J 4
                  ♦ 7 4 2
                  ♣ A 10 7 3
```

North	East	South	West
1♦	1♠	2NT	P
3NT		All Pass	

Opening Lead: ♠ King

Declarer, pleased with the opening lead, won the ace in dummy and started the diamonds. West won the king and played a spade. Whether declarer won or ducked now didn't matter.

The defenders continued spades. On the next diamond, East ran his winning spades.

How could South have played to make his contract?

The opening lead was friendly but a mirage. Declarer must duck and win the second spade.

As long as East does not have both the A-K of diamonds, declarer will win the race, getting nine before they get five.

3

DEAL 3. ENDPLAY DEFENDER IN FOUR SUITS

♠ J 10 4
♥ Q 8 4
♦ A 8 3
♣ J 10 7 4

♠ Q 9 3
♥ A 10 2
♦ K Q 10 9
♣ Q 8 3

♠ 6 5
♥ J 7 6 5
♦ 7 5 4
♣ K 9 6 5

♠ A K 8 7 2
♥ K 9 3
♦ J 6 2
♣ A 2

South opened 1♠ and passed North's raise to 2♠. Yes, 15 HCP, but 5332 distribution and poor spot cards. West led the ♦ king.

Declarer won the opening lead and had potential losers everywhere. After much agonizing and starring at the ceiling for inspiration she ended up losing one spade, two hearts, two diamonds, and one club. Down one. Not an easy hand.

Could you have done any better?

For starters it's always better for the declarer if the defense has to break suits than if you do yourself. Look at the difference if declarer ducks Trick 1.

What can West play next? Whatever doesn't matter. West has no escape and has to help declarer. It's going to be a one trick difference no matter what, but that's all she needs.

DEAL 4. DUCK, DANGER HAND

```
              ♠ A 7 3
              ♥ A J 7 4
              ♦ 6 3 2
              ♣ 10 9 2

  ♠ Q J 10 8              ♠ 9 6 5 4
  ♥ 6 3                   ♥ 5
  ♦ A Q 8                 ♦ J 10 9 5
  ♣ 8 6 4 3               ♣ K Q 7 5

              ♠ K 2
              ♥ K Q 10 9 8 2
              ♦ K 7 4
              ♣ A J
```

South opened 1♥ and bid 4♥ after North raised. West led the ♠Q.

Declarer won the opening lead in hand & drew trumps. Hoping to keep East off lead, he led a club; king from East, ace, six. When East won the second club, declarer lost three diamonds, down one.

Unlucky to find East with both club honors or was there a better line of play?

Declarer should duck the opening lead, keeping West on lead. Then win the next spade in hand, draw trumps & lead a club towards the A-J.

If East plays an honor, declarer wins the king, goes to dummy and discards the club jack on the spade ace.

Now a ruffing finesse keeps East off lead.

DEAL 5. DISRUPT COMMUNICATION

```
                    ♠ A 4
                    ♥ 10 8 5 2
                    ♦ Q J 10 7 3
                    ♣ A K

      ♠ 9 8 7 6                    ♠ Q J 10
      ♥ J 4                        ♥ A Q 9 7 6
      ♦ K 6                        ♦ 5 4
      ♣ 10 9 8 7 4                 ♣ J 6 5

                    ♠ K 5 3 2
                    ♥ K 3
                    ♦ A 9 8 2
                    ♣ Q 3 2
```

North	East	South	West
1♦	1♥	Dbl	P
2♦	P	3NT	All Pass

Opening Lead: ♥J

East encouraged with the seven and South won the king. He crossed to dummy and took a losing diamond finesse. Down one.

Was there a better line of play?

South forgot to listen to the bidding. East is certain to have five (or six) hearts for his overcall. South should duck the first trick. If West can lead another heart, East can win the ace & queen, but North's ten is a stopper.

When West wins the diamond king, South has the rest of the tricks.

DEAL 6. TWO DANGER HANDS ARE WORSE THAN ONE

♠ 5 4
♥ Q 7 4
♦ 6 5 4
♣ A K J 9 2

♠ 10 7 3   ♠ J 9 8 2
♥ J 9 6 5 3   ♥ K 10 8
♦ Q 9 8   ♦ K J 10
♣ 7 4   ♣ Q 6 5

♠ A K Q 6
♥ A 2
♦ A 7 3 2
♣ 10 8 3

South opened 1NT (almost too good?) and North raised to 3NT. West led the ♥5.

Declarer played the queen from dummy too quickly. East covered and South ducked, winning the next heart. When declarer lost the club finesse, the defense had four hearts and a club.

What was the proper play at Trick 1?

Declarer should play low from dummy and win the ace. By leaving Qx in the dummy, after losing the club finesse to East, the heart suit is safe and declarer has nine tricks.

He didn't need the queen as a trick to begin with. Again the ♥Q is a superfluous tenth trick, not a vital ninth. By preserving it, only West is the danger hand. If you play it at Trick 1 and East covers, both defenders become danger hands and there is no way to keep the danger hand out. Greed and speed kill.

DEAL 7. "HANDCUFF" THE OPPONENTS

```
            ♠ 7
            ♥ A 8
            ♦ K Q J 2
            ♣ Q 8 6 5 4 2

  ♠ 10 6 2              ♠ 5 4 3
  ♥ K Q J 9            ♥ 10 5 2
  ♦ 10 6 5 3           ♦ 9 8 7 4
  ♣ 10 9               ♣ K J 3

            ♠ A K Q J 9 8
            ♥ 7 6 4 3
            ♦ A
            ♣ A 7
```

South opened 1♠ and when North bid 2♣, game forcing, visions of slam of course danced in his head. He jumped to 3♠, by agreement setting trump. When North cue bid 4♥, he bid 6♠.

West led the ♥ King.

South had communication problems. After winning the heart ace, he had no entry to dummy other than ruffing a heart. But the defenders would win the second heart and play a trump.

Now declarer would lose three hearts and a club. Forget slam, down in game.

And the solution ?

Simple once you have seen it. Duck the first trick. What could the defense do? A simple way to look at it. Dummy has two entries for the defenders to dislodge. One is the ♥A, the other is the trump with which to ruff a second heart, which becomes an entry after dummy's low heart is gone.

So preserve the first entry while you establish the other, allowing the defenders to dislodge only one.

If West played a second heart, South would win the ace, play the diamond ace, ruff a heart and use the diamonds.

If at Trick 2 the defense played something else, declarer would draw trumps, unblock the diamond ace, and use the heart ace as an entry to the diamonds.

DEAL 8. LET THE OPPONENTS MAKE AN ERROR

```
                    ♠ 7 6
                    ♥ 5 3
                    ♦ K Q J 10 6
                    ♣ A 5 4 2

        ♠ Q 2                      ♠ 8 3
        ♥ A 10 8 2                 ♥ K J 9
        ♦ 8 5 2                    ♦ 9 7 4 3
        ♣ K Q J 10                 ♣ 9 8 7 6

                    ♠ A K J 10 9 5 4
                    ♥ Q 7 6 4
                    ♦ A
                    ♣ 3
```

West	North	East	South
1♣	1♦	P	4♠

Opening Lead: ♣ King

Declarer won the opening lead and led a heart, hoping 1) to ruff hearts in dummy and 2) the opponents were brain dead and would not switch to trumps.

He ended up with the nine tricks he started with, losing four heart tricks.

If I give you a mulligan, can you make four spades, maybe even make an overtrick?

Try the effect of casually ducking the opening lead. What would you play as West at Trick 2? Come on, tell the truth. Another club, why not? It's unlikely declarer has a singleton.

Now you can unblock the diamond ace on the club ace, dump four hearts on dummy's good diamonds as West ruffs the last one. Making five spades, losing only an unexpected club and spade.

Strange, not what you expected.

9

DEAL 9. AVOIDING DANGER

♠ K 6 4
♥ A J 8
♦ K 7 2
♣ K 6 4 2

♠ Q 10 3 2　　　　　　　　　♠ J 8 7 5
♥ 5 3　　　　　　　　　　　　♥ 7 6 2
♦ Q 9 6 3　　　　　　　　　　♦ A J 10
♣ Q 10 9　　　　　　　　　　♣ J 7 5

♠ A 9
♥ K Q 10 9 4
♦ 8 5 4
♣ A 8 3

North	South	
1♣	1♥	
1NT	2♦*	* Checkback
3♥^	4♥	^ Maximum with 3 hearts

Opening Lead: ♠ 2

Declarer needed to either set up a long club or find the diamond ace with West. He won the opening lead, drew trump & led the A-K of clubs and another club. But West won and shifted to a diamond. Down one.

Was there a better line of play?

West is the danger hand as we see above. Just duck the spade jack. If a spade is returned, win the ace, play the king, then ace of trumps & discard a club on the spade king. Play the ace, then king of clubs and ruff a club.

If they are 3-3, cross to the heart jack drawing the last trump and discard a diamond on the 13th club. If clubs are 4-2, ruff the club & lead towards the diamond king.

Ducking the first trick keeps the safe hand on lead.

DEAL 10. DANGER LURKS

♠ K Q 10
♥ A 6 5
♦ 6 4 3
♣ K 9 8 2

♠ 5 3   ♠ 9 6
♥ K Q 10 9   ♥ J 7 4 3 2
♦ A Q 9 8   ♦ J 10 5
♣ Q 10 5   ♣ J 7 6

♠ A J 8 7 4 2
♥ 8
♦ K 7 2
♣ A 4 3

North opened 1♣ and rebid 1NT after South's 1♠ response. South bid 4♠. West led the ♥K.

Declarer won the ace and drew trumps. If clubs were 3-3, he might discard a diamond as long as East did not win the third club.

He played the AK of clubs and a third club, but West had made a fine play, dropping the club queen under the king to allow East to win the third round.

When West turned up with the diamond ace, declarer was down one.

Good defense by West, but could declarer have prevailed?

Yes, in more than one way. Simplest and best? Duck the first heart, win a heart continuation with dummy's ♥A and discard a club. Then cash the ♠K and when both defenders follow, ruff dummy's last heart high.

Cash the ♣A, then a club to the king and ruff a club high. Cross to dummy's ♠10. When spades split 2-2, lead dummy's last club. If clubs divide 3-3, great.

If East shows out, discard a diamond. If West has the fourth club, he'll have no safe exit. He will either lead diamonds up to you or give you a ruff-sluff for your tenth trick.

DEAL 11. AVOIDING A SECOND ROUND RUFF

```
                        ♠ 10 6 4
                        ♥ K J 5 3
                        ♦ A Q 10 2
                        ♣ 8 2

        ♠ K J 9 5 3                        ♠ Q 8
        ♥ 8 4                              ♥ A Q 6
        ♦ 9 6 3                            ♦ 8 5 4
        ♣ Q 10 5                           ♣ J 9 7 6 4

                        ♠ A 7 2
                        ♥ 10 9 7 2
                        ♦ K J 7
                        ♣ A K 3
```

South	North
1NT	2♣
2♥	4♥
	All Pass

Opening Lead: ♠ 5

Declarer won the opening lead and led a trump. East won & returned a spade. West won and gave East a spade ruff. Down one.

Could declarer have done better?

With Axx opposite three low cards, it is almost always right to duck the first round. Since neither opponent bid, it's unlikely the side suit is divided 6-1.

By ducking the first round, when East wins the first trump, he has no way to reach West for a spade ruff.

The second spade loser is later discarded on dummy's fourth diamond, losing one spade and two trump tricks.

DEAL 12. TWELVE BECOMES ELEVEN

                    ♠ A K 9 8 3
                    ♥ A
                    ♦ 9 7 6 3
                    ♣ K 9 5

    ♠ Q   ♠ 10 6 5 2
    ♥ Q 10 8 7 5   ♥ K J 9 6 4 3 2
    ♦ K J 10   ♦ Q 4
    ♣ 8 7 3 2   ♣ void

                    ♠ J 7 4
                    ♥ void
                    ♦ A 8 5 2
                    ♣ A Q J 10 6 4

North opened 1♠ and South bid 2♣. North raised to 3♣ and South bid 3♦. Was this a cue bid or an attempt to reach 3NT? North bid 3NT, but South continued with 4♥, making it apparent that he was not looking for 3NT. When North bid 4♠, South bid 6♣. West led the ♣Q.

Declarer won the opening lead. But when East showed out on the first round of trumps, South was in trouble. Continuing trumps would lead to eleven tricks; trying to set up the spades first would result in a ruff.

Unlucky or could South have made her slam?

The opening lead certainly is a singleton. If declarer simply counts her tricks and makes a somewhat unusual but not unreasonable play at Trick 1 by ducking the spade queen, she has twelve tricks. Six clubs, four spades, and two red aces.

"I should have led a diamond," moaned West.

DEAL 13. WHAT CAN GO WRONG?

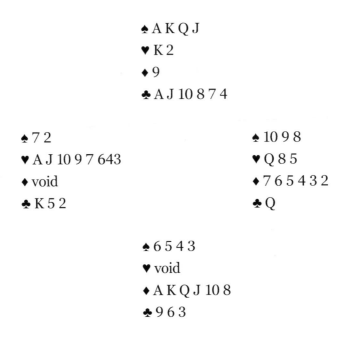

```
                    ♠ A K Q J
                    ♥ K 2
                    ♦ 9
                    ♣ A J 10 8 7 4

    ♠ 7 2                               ♠ 10 9 8
    ♥ A J 10 9 7 643                    ♥ Q 8 5
    ♦ void                              ♦ 7 6 5 4 3 2
    ♣ K 5 2                             ♣ Q

                    ♠ 6 5 4 3
                    ♥ void
                    ♦ A K Q J 10 8
                    ♣ 9 6 3
```

West	North	East	South
4♥	5♣	5♥	6♦
			All Pass

Opening Lead: ♥ Ace

Declarer ruffed the opening lead and led the diamond ace. When West showed out, South said to himself "I forgot to ask myself what could go wrong." Twelve tricks became eleven, losing a diamond and a club.

"Partner," asked North. "Didn't you read Jim and Danny's book entitled L O L?"

West had made the only lead to let South make 6♦. How?

When West led the ♥A, South could count twelve tricks: six diamonds, four spades, the ♣A and the ♥K. When he ruffed and led the ♦A, however West showed out. Now South was unable to draw East's last trump. East ruffed dummy's last spade. Four spade tricks became three.

Declarer has twelve tricks despite a 6-0 trump split as long as he doesn't lose control. Just duck the heart ace, discarding one club loser now and the other club loser later on the heart king, loser-on-loser plays.

DEAL 14. KEEP YOUR TEN TRICKS INTACT

$$\spadesuit Q\,8\,5$$
$$\heartsuit J\,2$$
$$\diamondsuit K\,Q\,7\,3$$
$$\clubsuit K\,8\,7\,4$$

♠ 6 4		♠ 10 9 7 3
♥ 8 7 5 4 3		♥ 6
♦ 9 8 4 2		♦ A J 10 6 5
♣ 10 9		♣ A Q J

$$\spadesuit A\,K\,J\,2$$
$$\heartsuit A\,K\,Q\,10\,9$$
$$\diamondsuit \text{void}$$
$$\clubsuit 6\,5\,3\,2$$

East	South	West	North
1♦	Dbl	P	2NT
P	3♥	P	3NT
P	4♥	All Pass	

Opening Lead: ♦ 2

Declarer played the diamond king, East the ace, and South ruffed. South started the trumps, but East discarded on the 2nd round. With nothing else to do, declarer cashed his trumps & started spades. West ruffed the third round & led a diamond. Dummy's queen was declarer's last trick.

"Partner," said North. "I thought we just went over this."

Down two.

Was there a better line of play?

Declarer started with ten tricks: five hearts, four spades, and one diamond. To maintain control & guard against a 5-1 trump break, declarer should discard a club at Trick 1, another loser-on-loser.

DEAL 15. DUCKING FOR DECEPTION

```
                        ♠ 9 6
                        ♥ 5 3
                        ♦ K 7 2
                        ♣ K 9 8 7 4 2

       ♠ 8 5 4                        ♠ A 3
       ♥ K Q 7 6                      ♥ J 10 9 8
       ♦ A 8 6                        ♦ 5 4 3
       ♣ Q 10 6                       ♣ A J 5 3

                        ♠ K Q J 10 7 2
                        ♥ A 7 2
                        ♦ Q J 10 9
                        ♣ void
```

South opened 1♠ and North bid 1NT, forcing for one round. South bid 2♦ and North made a simple preference to 2♠. South fell in love with his hand and bid 4♠.

West led the ♥K.

Declarer with four losers, two hearts, one spade, and one diamond, won the opening lead and needing to ruff a heart immediately played one back.

The defenders played two rounds of trumps, down one.

Could declarer have done better?

Maybe. If declarer casually ducks the first trick, if the opponents don't play two rounds of trumps next, declarer is making four spades.

DEAL 16. SAVE AN ENTRY

♠ Q 5
♥ A Q 4
♦ J 7 2
♣ K 9 6 3 2

♠ 3 2   ♠ 6 4
♥ J 9 7 5 3   ♥ K 10 8
♦ K 8 5 3   ♦ Q 9 6 4
♣ 7 4   ♣ Q J 10 8

♠ A K J 10 9 8 7
♥ 6 2
♦ A 10
♣ A 5

North opened 1♣ and South bid 2♠, an Old-Fashioned Strong Jump Shift. When North bid 3♥, South asked for Keycards and settled for 6♠. West led the ♥ 5.

Declarer played the heart queen, a little too quickly perhaps. East won and returned a heart forcing out the ace. With clubs 4-2, declarer was now one entry shy of setting up the last club for a diamond discard.

Down one.

Could South have done better? Do you want another mulligan?

South needed to preserve her entry so she should play a low heart from dummy at Trick 1.

East cannot return a heart so now declarer can proceed with setting up the clubs.

She can win the diamond return, cash the A-K of clubs and ruff a club. Then the A-Q of trumps, club ruff and the heart ace is the entry to the good club.

DEAL 17. ENTRIES

```
                    ♠ 7 6 5
                    ♥ J 10
                    ♦ Q 3 2
                    ♣ A K 6 5 2

        ♠ K 9 4                      ♠ Q J 8 3
        ♥ A 9 7 6 3                  ♥ Q 8 5 4 2
        ♦ 4                          ♦ 7 6
        ♣ J 10 9 8                   ♣ Q 4

                    ♠ A 10 2
                    ♥ K
                    ♦ A K J 10 9 8 5
                    ♣ 7 3
```

South	West	North	East
1♦	P	1NT	P
3♦	P	4♦	P
5♦	All Pass		

Opening Lead: ♣ Jack

South won the opening lead, drew trumps, led a club to the king & ruffed a club hoping for a 3/3 club division.

When East discarded, South had two spade losers and one heart loser for down one. Was there a better line of play?

The problem was entries to set up the clubs. What if South ducked the first trick!

What could West do? If West shifted to a trump, declarer could win the A-K of trumps, cash the A-K of clubs and ruff a club.

The diamond queen would be the entry to the good club.

18

DEAL 18. DUCK, DUCK, DUCK

♠ Q J 2
♥ A K J
♦ Q J 5 4
♣ A 7 2

♠ 5 3   ♠ K 10 9 8 7
♥ 9 6 4   ♥ 8 7 3 2
♦ K 8 3   ♦ A 7
♣ K 10 9 6 5   ♣ 8 4

♠ A 6 4
♥ Q 10 5
♦ 10 9 6 2
♣ Q J 3

East	South	West	North
P	P	P	1♦
1♠	1NT	P	2NT
P	3NT		
All Pass			

Opening Lead: ♠ 5

South played the spade queen, East ducked to keep communication. When South started the diamonds, West won, continued spades and eventually declarer finished down one.

How could declarer have done better?

Duck & duck. South can "freeze" the suit by playing low at Trick 1. East plays the seven, winning, & shifts to a club. The same layout. South plays low again. West wins but that suit is "frozen."

The defense could get two diamonds, one spade, and one club.

19

DEAL 19. DANGER HAND

```
                        ♠ 8 5
                        ♥ A 2
                        ♦ A J 9 8 6 4
                        ♣ Q 9 4

        ♠ A 7 4                        ♠ Q J 10 2
        ♥ K Q J 7 4                    ♥ 9 8 6 5 3
        ♦ 3 2                          ♦ K 10 7
        ♣ 5 3 2                        ♣ 8

                        ♠ K 9 6 3
                        ♥ 10
                        ♦ Q 5
                        ♣ A K J 10 7 6
```

South	West	North	East
1♣	1♥	2♦	3♥
4♣	P	5♣	All Pass

Opening Lead: ♥ King

South won the ace of hearts, drew trumps, took a losing diamond finesse, and when East returned the queen of spades, lost two spades for down one.

Could South have done better?

South went down at Trick 1. What type of hand is this? Actually two types, a danger hand and a second suit. South needed to set up the diamonds without letting East in for the spade switch.

How could he do this?

Just duck the opening lead, keeping West, the safe hand on lead. Win Trick 2, then discard a diamond on the heart ace. Now it was a simple matter of setting up the diamonds without letting East in.

DEAL 20. ANOTHER DANGER HAND

♠ 2
♥ A Q J 10 7 6 4
♦ K 4 3
♣ J 3

♠ 9   ♠ 8 6 5 4
♥ 8 2   ♥ K 5
♦ 10 7 6 5 2   ♦ A Q J
♣ Q 9 8 7 2   ♣ K 6 5 4

♠ A K Q J 10 7 3
♥ 9 3
♦ 9 8
♣ A 10

South opened 1♠ and North bid 2♥. South's 3♠ rebid set trump, but did not show any extra strength. North made one cue bid of 4♥ and South signed off in 4♠. West led the ♣7.

South won the opening lead and drew trumps. He then took a losing heart finesse. East returned a club to West's queen, and the diamond switch resulted in two more tricks for E/W.

Down one.

Could South have made this contract?

All South had to do was duck the opening lead. West was the danger hand, not East.

If East won the heart finesse, declarer has ten tricks.

If East ducked, South has an interesting problem.

DEAL 21. DISRUPTING COMMUNICATION

```
                          ♠ 10 5 3 2
                          ♥ A K
                          ♦ 10 9 8 4 3
                          ♣ A K

        ♠ Q 6                              ♠ A J 9 8 4
        ♥ 6 5 3 2                          ♥ 10 8 7 4
        ♦ K 5 2                            ♦ 6
        ♣ 9 6 5 3                          ♣ Q J 10

                          ♠ K 7
                          ♥ Q J 9
                          ♦ A Q J 7
                          ♣ 8 7 4 2
```

North opened 1♦ and East overcalled 1♠. South bid 3NT.

West led the ♠Q. Declarer won the opening lead after East encouraged with the nine. He led a heart to dummy and returned the ten of diamonds, expecting the finesse to succeed, West won the king and returned a spade. East took four spade tricks for down one.

Unlucky or poor technique?

South can succeed by ducking the first trick. If West led another spade, East's ace drops South's king, but the 10-5 in dummy still would provide a stopper.

When West wins the diamond king, he has no spade to return.

DEAL 22. UNMAKEABLE CONTRACT, BUT…

                                    ♠ Q J 2
                                    ♥ K 7 2
                                    ♦ J 10 6
                                    ♣ 8 6 5 2

            ♠ 7 5 4   ♠ 8 3
            ♥ J 10 9 5   ♥ Q 8 6 3
            ♦ A Q 7   ♦ K 8 4 3
            ♣ J 7 4   ♣ Q 10 9

                                    ♠ A K 10 9 6
                                    ♥ A 4
                                    ♦ 9 5 2
                                    ♣ A K 3

South opened 1♠ and North raised to 2♠. South bid 4♠ and West led the ♥J.

Declarer is looking at four losers: three diamonds and a club.

Is the contract doomed?

Probably, but a little deception goes a long way. When East plays an encouraging eight of hearts at Trick 1, look at the effect of declarer ducking. West will probably continue the suit.

Now South wins, cashes the ace of trumps, the AK of clubs and goes to dummy's jack of trumps.

Now he discards his last club on the heart king, ruffs a club, & when the clubs split 3-3, draws the last trump with the queen.

He discards a diamond loser on the thirteenth club.

DEAL 23. UNUSUAL DANGER HAND

```
                    ♠ Q 8
                    ♥ 4 2
                    ♦ A K J 6 5 4
                    ♣ Q J 3

        ♠ K 6 2                       ♠ 5 4
        ♥ A 10 7 6                    ♥ 9 8
        ♦ 9 2                         ♦ Q 10 8 7
        ♣ 10 9 7 4                    ♣ A K 6 5 2

                    ♠ A J 10 9 7 3
                    ♥ K Q J 5 3
                    ♦ 3
                    ♣ 8
```

South	West	North	East
1♠	P	2♦	P
2♥	P	3♦	P
3♥	P	3♠	P
4♠		AllPass	

West led the ♣10.

Declarer played the queen, East won the king & shifted to a trump. West won & returned a trump.

South won, drew the last trump & led the heart king. He ruffed the club return.

When hearts did not split, he tried a diamond finesse in desperation for a heart discard. Down two.

Unlucky or misplayed?

What kind of deal is this? Hard to recognize but a danger hand.

South needs to ruff at least one heart and can't afford a trump switch. If he plays low at Trick 1, West can't effectively lead trumps twice from his side.

So South can ruff a heart in dummy or West loses his spade trick.

And if East overtakes at Trick 1, declarer can build his tenth trick with the Q-J of clubs in dummy.

DEAL 24. AN UNUSUAL DUCK

                    ♠ K 5
                    ♥ Q 4
                    ♦ J 7 5 2
                    ♣ Q J 10 7 3

    ♠ 9 8   ♠ J 10 7 4 3
    ♥ 9 7 6   ♥ J 10 8 2
    ♦ Q 9 8 6 3   ♦ K 4
    ♣ K 5 2   ♣ A 6

                    ♠ A Q 6 2
                    ♥ A K 5 3
                    ♦ A 10
                    ♣ 9 8 4

South opened 1NT and North bid 3NT.

Opening Lead: ♦6

West led a 4th best diamond, East played the king. How should South play? It looked logical to win the ace since South now has two diamond tricks, five tricks in the majors, and start the clubs.

Are there any problems?

East will win the first club and return a diamond to West's queen who will continue the suit. When West gets in with the club king, he will cash two more diamonds for down one.

How should South have played?

Even though winning the diamond ace assured two diamond tricks, that was not necessary. South only needed one diamond trick, five major tricks, and three club tricks.

The danger was that if West had five diamonds plus an entry, it was necessary to let East's king win the first trick. South could then win the diamond return. When East wins the club, he must shift and South has time to set up the clubs for nine tricks before the defenders can take five.

DEAL 25. PROTECTING YOUR TRUMPS

```
                    ♠ A K J
                    ♥ 3
                    ♦ 9 8 7 4
                    ♣ A Q J 8 7

    ♠ 3                            ♠ 10 9 8 7
    ♥ K Q 10 8                     ♥ 9 7 6 5
    ♦ Q 10 6 5 3                   ♦ K J 2
    ♣ 6 4 3                        ♣ K 9

                    ♠ Q 6 5 4 2
                    ♥ A J 4 2
                    ♦ A
                    ♣ 10 5 2
```

South reached 4♠ after responding 1♠, then making a natural 3♥ game try after North bid 2♠. North had a maximum to only bid 2♠, but the lack of any low spades with which to ruff hearts negated his ruffing values, leaving little in the way of alternatives. He was certainly pleased South bid again.

The opening lead was the ♥ King.

Declarer won the heart ace and took a club finesse. East won and returned a heart, ruffed in dummy. Declarer cashed the A-K of spades and found he had a trump loser.

He came to hand with the diamond ace to cash the trump queen.

But when he tried to run the clubs, East ruffed in too soon and declarer lost two more heart tricks.

Was there a way to play to protect those spades?

If declarer ducks the opening lead, he does not have to ruff a heart in dummy. After winning a diamond shift, he can cash all three of dummy's trump honors and lead towards his ♣10. This play guarantees his contract, probably with an overtrick.

DEAL 26. AN UNUSUAL DUCK

                    ♠ K J 8 6
                    ♥ 5 3
                    ♦ K Q
                    ♣ 10 9 6 5 3

    ♠ 10 3   ♠ 9 2
    ♥ K J 10 9 6 2   ♥ 8 7 4
    ♦ A J 10 7   ♦ 9 8 6 4 3
    ♣ Q   ♣ K J 7

                    ♠ A Q 7 5 4
                    ♥ A Q
                    ♦ 5 2
                    ♣ A 8 4 2

South	West	North	East
1♠	2♥	2♠	P
3♣	P	4♠	All Pass

Opening Lead: ♣ Queen

Declarer won the opening lead and drew trumps. As Frank Stewart says, "if you are going to make a poor decision by playing too fast, the first trick is a good time."

Declarer next led a club. East won and led a heart. The finesse lost, and South still had two more losers.

Down one.

Was there a better line of play? What kind of deal is this?

A second suit deal. The road to success is to leave West, the safe hand, on lead at Trick 1. Losing a club trick early to the defender who cannot harm you instead of later to the danger hand has to be right. West can't lead a heart. West played ace and a diamond. After getting in with the second diamond, declarer can draw trumps. Then the ♣A and another club in time to set up a discard for the ♥Q.

No heart finesse needed, thank you.

DEAL 27. AN UNFAMILIAR GUISE

♠ A 4 2
♥ K Q 9
♦ Q 10 8 3 2
♣ Q 5

♠ K 9 8 6 5   ♠ J 3
♥ J 8 6   ♥ 10 7 4 3
♦ A 7   ♦ K 6 5
♣ 10 8 6   ♣ K 7 4 2

♠ Q 10 7
♥ A 5 2
♦ J 9 4
♣ A J 9 3

South opened 1♣ and rebid 1NT after North's 1♦ response. North bid 3NT.

West led the ♠6.

Dummy played low and East played the jack. Declarer won the queen and started setting up the diamonds.

East won the diamond king and returned a spade; ten, king, ace. When West won the next diamond, he cashed the spades. Down one.

How could this have been avoided?

Unless West had an unlikely king-fifth in spades and both top diamonds, he could not get in often enough to both establish and cash enough winners to defeat the contract. All South needed to do was let East win the ♠J at Trick 1. East might continue spades but would have no more upon winning a top diamond.

The holdup at Trick I was essential if the diamond honors were split. If West then won the first diamond, he could not attack spades.

If East won the first diamond, he would have no spade to return.

DEAL 28. SPOT CARDS MEAN A LOT

                    ♠ 9 6 2
                    ♥ A J 10 6 3
                    ♦ 4 2
                    ♣ K J 3

    ♠ Q J 5 4 3   ♠ K 10
    ♥ 8 2   ♥ K Q 7 5 4
    ♦ J 7 6 5   ♦ A Q 10 8 3
    ♣ 6 4   ♣ 7

                    ♠ A 8 7
                    ♥ 9
                    ♦ K 9
                    ♣ A Q 10 9 8 5 2

East	South	West	North
1♥	2♣	P	3♣
3♦	3♠	4♦	P
P	5♣	All	Pass

Opening Lead: ♥ 8

Declarer won the heart ace and drew trumps. He led a diamond from dummy and lost one diamond and two spade tricks. Not much of an effort.

Was the contract too high or was there a way home?

Look closely at the heart spot cards.

Duck the opening lead, East can win an honor but cannot continue hearts. There is only one card higher than the N/S spots. After East wins Trick 1, a ruffing finesse against his remaining high honor will allow dummy's ♥AJ provide discards for the spade losers.

Seven clubs, two hearts, the spade ace and the easily establishable ♦K will give South eleven tricks.

Spot cards mean a lot. Pay attention to them.

DEAL 29. PROMOTE YOUR SPOT CARDS

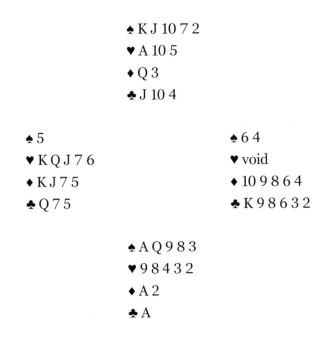

```
                    ♠ K J 10 7 2
                    ♥ A 10 5
                    ♦ Q 3
                    ♣ J 10 4

        ♠ 5                         ♠ 6 4
        ♥ K Q J 7 6                 ♥ void
        ♦ K J 7 5                   ♦ 10 9 8 6 4
        ♣ Q 7 5                     ♣ K 9 8 6 3 2

                    ♠ A Q 9 8 3
                    ♥ 9 8 4 3 2
                    ♦ A 2
                    ♣ A
```

South	West	North	East
1♠	2♥	3♥	P
4♠		All Pass	

Opening Lead: ♥ K

Declarer played dummy's ace of hearts, East ruffed and returned a diamond.
South ended losing one spade, two hearts and a diamond. Down one.
Could declarer have done better?

Sure, declarer knew East was void in hearts. South need only duck the first heart honor and the second, if West persists, This keeps East, the danger hand, when the auction suggests West has the ♦K, from getting in early. When East ruffs the third heart and returns a diamond, South wins his ace.

Now the stage is set to draw trumps and use his remaining ♥98 to take a ruffing finesse thru West's remaining honor. His now high precious good heart spot can be used to dump dummy's diamond loser.

DEAL 30. NIL DESPERANDUM

$\spadesuit$ J 8 5
$\heartsuit$ J 4 2
$\diamondsuit$ K 7 3
$\clubsuit$ 6 5 3 2

$\spadesuit$ K 9 6 2 $\spadesuit$ A Q 10 4 3
$\heartsuit$ 6 $\heartsuit$ 7 5
$\diamondsuit$ Q J 10 6 2 $\diamondsuit$ 9 8 5
$\clubsuit$ Q 9 4 $\clubsuit$ J 10 7

$\spadesuit$ 7
$\heartsuit$ A K Q 10 98 3
$\diamondsuit$ A 4
$\clubsuit$ A K 8

South	North
2$\clubsuit$	2$\diamondsuit$
2$\heartsuit$	3$\heartsuit$
6$\heartsuit$	All Pass

Opening Lead: $\diamondsuit$ Q

Declarer won the opening lead, drew trumps and played off his winners. But in the end he could not avoid losing a spade and a club. Down one

How would you play to make six hearts? Was there any hope for this contract?

No, not really but what if you smoothly ducked the opening lead. West may not know you are missing the $\spadesuit$A and might just continue diamonds. Now you can win the $\diamondsuit$A, cash the $\heartsuit$A and the two top clubs.

Then lead the $\heartsuit$10 to dummy's $\heartsuit$J to pitch a low club on dummy's $\diamondsuit$K and ruff a club high. The carefully preserved $\heartsuit$3 to dummy's $\heartsuit$4 is your entry to the thirteenth club and away goes your spade loser.

DEAL 31. COMMUNICATION PROBLEMS

       ♠ 5 4 3
       ♥ K Q 7
       ♦ A J 7 2
       ♣ 8 6 2

♠ Q J 2   ♠ K 9 8 7
♥ 5 3   ♥ A 9 2
♦ K Q 10 9   ♦ 6 5 3
♣ J 10 4 3   ♣ 9 7 5

       ♠ A 10 6
       ♥ J 10 8 6 4
       ♦ 8 4
       ♣ A K Q

South opened 1♥ and after North showed a limit raise with three trumps, overbid a bit and bid 4 ♥.

 The opening lead was the ♦ King.

 South won the first diamond and played a club to his hand. He led a diamond, West winning the queen and now South had a good diamond in dummy. West switched to a spade.

 The good diamond is still sitting in dummy as you read this, the defense taking two spades, one diamond and the trump ace. Declarer had no way to get to dummy in time.

 Could you find a way to use that good diamond?

 South needs a way to reach the dummy. Easy, duck the first trick. Declarer can win the spade switch and lead his last diamond, take a finesse, and now can discard one of his spade losers.

DEAL 32. DUCKING IN A SUIT CONTRACT

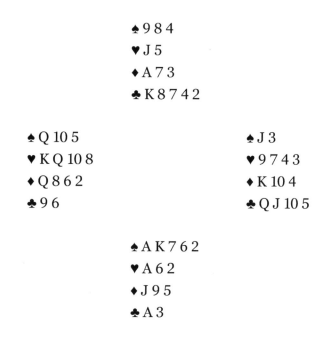

♠ 9 8 4
♥ J 5
♦ A 7 3
♣ K 8 7 4 2

♠ Q 10 5
♥ K Q 10 8
♦ Q 8 6 2
♣ 9 6

♠ J 3
♥ 9 7 4 3
♦ K 10 4
♣ Q J 10 5

♠ A K 7 6 2
♥ A 6 2
♦ J 9 5
♣ A 3

South opened 1♠ and after North raised, bid 4♠. West led the ♥K.

Declarer won the ace and cashed the AK of trumps. He cashed the AK of clubs and ruffed a club as West discarded rather than overruff.

Declarer led a heart and West won the queen and cashed the queen of trumps. After cashing his heart ten, declarer still had two diamond losers. Down two.

How would you have managed these assets to bring home four spades?

A little duck and a little bit of luck will do it. Duck at Trick 1, losing a trick early rather than late to retain control. Win the heart continuation and cash both top trumps. Then ruff out the clubs using a heart ruff as an entry to lead dummy's fourth club.

West can overruff or not, but regardless, dummy's ♦A remains as an entry to let declarer discard a diamond loser on the fifth club. Ten tricks.

DEAL 33. IT FEELS RIGHT

♠ A K
♥ K 10 6 3
♦ 8 7 2
♣ K 10 8 4

♠ J 9 2   ♠ Q 10 7 5 4
♥ 7   ♥ A Q 4
♦ Q J 10 6   ♦ K 9 5 3
♣ J 9 7 6 5   ♣ 3

♠ 8 6 3
♥ J 9 8 5 2
♦ A 4
♣ A Q 2

North opened 1♣ and South bid 1♥. When North bid 2♥, South bid 4♥.

The opening lead was the ♦ Queen.

Declarer won the ace at Trick 1 and led a trump to East's queen. East returned his singleton club. He won the next trump, underled in diamonds to West's jack and got a club ruff. Down one.

Could you make four hearts with the same lead?

Good bridge instincts help here. You can afford to lose two trump tricks and one diamond and still make your contract. Duck the first diamond and win the second. The play will continue the same as above, but East can never get West back in for the club ruff.

When South ducks, does he foresee the whole hand and play? No, it's probable instinctive, but that's the mark of an expert.

DEAL 34. ONLY LOSING OPTIONS

```
                      ♠ 3
                      ♥ A 8
                      ♦ K Q 6 5 4 2
                      ♣ 7 5 3 2

    ♠ 10 6 4                          ♠ 9 5
    ♥ K Q 10 7                        ♥ 9 5 4 2
    ♦ A J 3                           ♦ 10 9 8
    ♣ K J 4                           ♣ 10 9 8 6

                      ♠ A K Q J 8 7 2
                      ♥ J 6 3
                      ♦ 7
                      ♣ A Q
```

South open 1♠, North bid 1NT and South bid 4 ♠.

West led the: ♥ King.

Declarer counted winners: one heart, one heart ruff, seven spades, one diamond, one club. But not so fast. How many losers? Declarer won the ace and played back a heart.

The defense played a trump. No heart ruff for you. Declarer later led a diamond. The defenders took their ace. No diamond for you. Eleven became nine, down one. Very sad.

Is this contract hopeless or was there a way home?

If declarer ducks Trick 1, the defenders have only two losing options. Switch to a trump which stops the ruff but leaves an entry to the diamond later. Or continue hearts which kills the entry but allows the ruff.

Ten tricks either way.

DEAL 35. SECOND SUIT BUT DANGER LURKS

```
                    ♠ 7 4
                    ♥ A 9
                    ♦ Q 10 2
                    ♣ A 9 8 7 6 5

        ♠ A 6 5                      ♠ Q J 10 9
        ♥ K Q J 10 8                 ♥ 7 5 4 3 2
        ♦ 7 5 3                      ♦ 6
        ♣ 10 4                       ♣ K Q J

                    ♠ K 8 3 2
                    ♥ 6
                    ♦ A K J 9 8 4
                    ♣ 3 2
```

South	West	North	East
1♦	1♥	2♣	2♥
2♠	P	5♦	All Pass

Opening lead: ♥ King

Declarer won the heart ace. The plan was to set up the club suit. The danger was East would win the second club and lead a spade thru declarer's king.

Of course, that's exactly what happened, down one.

Was there a better line of play?

This is a typical danger hand deal, East being the danger hand. Duck the opening lead.

West can't attack spades.

Now declarer can discard a club on the heart ace and set up the clubs without giving up the lead.

DEAL 36. AN UNUSUAL SUIT COMBINATION

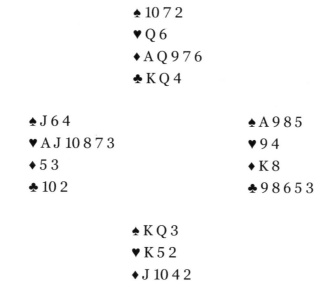

♠ 10 7 2
♥ Q 6
♦ A Q 9 7 6
♣ K Q 4

♠ J 6 4
♥ A J 10 8 7 3
♦ 5 3
♣ 10 2

♠ A 9 8 5
♥ 9 4
♦ K 8
♣ 9 8 6 5 3

♠ K Q 3
♥ K 5 2
♦ J 10 4 2
♣ A J 7

South	West	North	East
1♦	2♥	3♥	P
3NT		All Pass	

Opening Lead: ♥ J

The normal way to play this combination is play the queen from dummy, keeping the guarded king. That's what South did and when he took a diamond finesse into East, back came a heart and down went the contract.

Was there a better line of play?

Are you getting tired of hearing this question?

This is another typical danger hand deal. South needs to make the unusual play of ducking Trick 1. West can continue with ace and another heart but when East wins his diamond, South has his contract if West does not have the spade ace.

Bridge is not a game of rules you read in a book. As Mike Lawrence once said, "I don't know any book that ever won a bridge tournament."

DEAL 37. QUACK, QUACK, QUACK

♠ K 9 6 3
♥ A 10
♦ A 5
♣ A 6 5 3 2

♠ A Q 8 7 5 4 2
♥ 9 5
♦ J
♣ 10 8 4

North	East	South	West	
1♣	2NT*	3♠	P	*Two-suited: Hearts & Diamonds
4♠		All Pass		

Opening Lead: ♣ King

Declarer played the ace at Trick 1, ruffed by East. He later lost two clubs and a heart, down one.

How should declarer have assured his contract?

Warned by the bidding to protect his ten tricks, he should duck the first three club tricks. After that he has no problem and can throw his heart loser on the club ace.

East's hand: ♠ 10   ♥ K J 7 6 4 2   ♦ K Q 9 7 6 3   ♣ void

DEAL 38. LOW, LOW, LOW WE GO

♠ Q 7
♥ Q J 4
♦ Q 10 8 5 3
♣ 8 5 2

♠ J 8 6 5 4 3 2   ♠ 9
♥ 8 3   ♥ K 10 9 7 5
♦ K 4   ♦ A 7
♣ 7 4   ♣ K 10 9 6 3

♠ A K 10
♥ A 6 2
♦ J 9 6 2
♣ A Q J

South	West	North	East
1♦	2♠	P	P
2NT	P	3NT	All Pass

Opening lead: ♥ 8

Declarer played the queen, East encouraged with the ten. Declarer led a diamond, West winning the king. He led his last heart, forcing out declarer's ace.

When East got in with the diamond ace, declarer was down one.

How should declarer play?

If East has both the A-K of diamonds, declarer cannot make 3NT. But if the honors are divided, declarer must play low from both hands at Trick 1. West leads his second heart, queen, king, ace.

When West wins his diamond, he cannot continue hearts and declarer has time to set up the diamonds.

DEAL 39. SAVE THAT ACE

♠ A 10 8 6 5 4 2
♥ void
♦ K J 10
♣ Q 8 5

♠ K Q J 9 3   ♠ void
♥ K J 10 5   ♥ A 9 6 4
♦ 7 4   ♦ 9 8 6 5 3 2
♣ 9 3   ♣ 10 6 2

♠ 7
♥ Q 8 7 3 2
♦ A Q
♣ A K J 7 4

South	West	North	East
1♥	1♠	P	P
2♣	P	3NT	P
4♣	P	5♣	All Pass

Opening Lead: ♠ K

Perhaps South should have re-opened with a double instead of bidding two clubs? Anyhow, South played the ace, East ruffed and returned a trump. South took five trumps in hand, two heart ruffs in the dummy and three diamonds, ten tricks for down one. No spade ace.

Could South have done better? Would a trump lead always defeat the contract?

If South ducks the first trick, the defense will shift to a trump. But now South can take the same ten tricks as above PLUS the spade ace later.

An initial trump lead is the same ten tricks PLUS the spade ace.

DEAL 40. BREAKING COMMUNICATION

♠ K 9
♥ A 8
♦ J 8 7 3 2
♣ Q J 10 6

♠ 10 8 6 5   ♠ A Q 4 3 2
♥ Q 9 5 4   ♥ K 10 6
♦ 6   ♦ K Q 10
♣ 8 5 3 2   ♣ 9 7

♠ J 7
♥ J 7 3 2
♦ A 9 5 4
♣ A K 4

South	West	North	East
1♦	P	3♦*	All Pass

• Invitational

Opening Lead: ♥4

Declarer won the opening lead in dummy with the ace and started the trumps. He led to the ace and then to dummy. East could count two trump winners, one heart, and needed to get West in to lead a spade to get two spade winners.

Since South would probably have played low at Trick 1 if he had the queen, East returned a low heart from his king. West got the message. His spade return got the job done. Down one.

Can you see a possible better line of play?

East's reasoning was reasonable. But South should duck Trick 1 to avoid exactly what happened. He cannot guarantee his contract but having East on lead is certainly better.

He can hope to later discard a spade on the long club.

41

DEAL 41. DUCKING IN A 4-3 FIT

```
              ♠ 6
              ♥ Q 8 7
              ♦ 7 6 5 4
              ♣ A K Q J 10

   ♠ K Q 10                    ♠ J 9 8 7 3
   ♥ 5 3                       ♥ A 6 4 2
   ♦ K 10 8 3 2                ♦ J 9
   ♣ 5 3 2                     ♣ 6 4

              ♠ A 5 4 2
              ♥ K J 10 9
              ♦ A Q
              ♣ 9 8 7
```

North	East	South	West
1♣	P	1♥	P
2♥	P	2NT*	P
3♦^	P	4♥	All Pass

South's 2NT was forcing, asking for more description.

3♦ showed a maximum raise, three trumps, and shortness somewhere. West led the ♠ King.

Declarer won the opening lead, ruffed a spade, returned to the ace of diamonds and ruffed another spade. South then tried drawing trumps. East won the third round, cashed another spade and played another spade, leaving declarer with no trumps. East ruffed the third club, scoring two hearts, one spade and one diamond for down one.

Was there a better line of play?

If declarer ducks the opening lead, seemingly counterintuitive with the ace facing a singleton, the defense is helpless. West can continue the suit but now declarer can ruff in dummy and play on trumps. If the defense plays another spade, declarer wins the ace and gets home with an overtrick.

DEAL 42. DUCK THEN ELIMINATE

♠ Q J 9 8 3 2
♥ J 10 4
♦ A 6 4
♣ 5

♠ 6 4
♥ K Q 8 3
♦ J 8 5
♣ K Q 10 4

♠ 5
♥ 7 5 2
♦ K Q 9 3
♣ 8 7 6 3 2

♠ A K 10 7
♥ A 9 6
♦ 10 7 3
♣ A J 9

South opened 1NT and North bid 4♥, a Texas transfer to 4♠.

West led the ♣ K.

South won the opening lead, ruffed a club, drew trumps, & ruffed his last club. He then led the heart jack to finesse, West winning and returning a diamond, ducked to the queen. East led another heart. South lost another finesse, and later another diamond for down one.

Was there a better line of play?

What kind of deal is this? Lots of trumps - think elimination. Duck the first trick! Say West shifts to a diamond. South takes the ace, leads a trump to his hand, and discards dummy's last two diamonds on the A-J of clubs.

West has now won two tricks. If he returns his last trump, South wins, ruffs a diamond, leads a trump to his hand and ruffs his last diamond. Having completed the elimination of the minors, he leads the jack of hearts for a losing finesse. West is endplayed.

DEAL 43. CUTTING A LINK

```
                    ♠ 7 5 4
                    ♥ A Q J 3
                    ♦ J 10 9 4 3
                    ♣ A

    ♠ K Q J 10 3                    ♠ 9 2
    ♥ 9 8 2                         ♥ K 10 7 6
    ♦ 5                             ♦ 6 2
    ♣ K J 7 6                       ♣ Q 10 8 5 3

                    ♠ A 8 6
                    ♥ 5 4
                    ♦ A K Q 8 7
                    ♣ 9 4 2
```

South	West	North	East
1♦	1♠	Dbl	P
2♦	P	5♦	All Pass

Opening Lead: ♠ King

Declarer won the opening lead, drew trumps and took a losing heart finesse. East returned a spade. Down one.

How should declarer have played?

How many spades do you think West has? Five? Six? With a six-card suit and a weak hand, most would have made a weak jump overcall. With a better hand, West might have bid two spades over two diamonds.

So West probably has five spades. Duck the opening lead and win the second spade. Now when East wins the heart king, he has no spade to return. South can discard his spade loser on the good heart.

Ducking with A-x-x-(x) facing x-x is almost always right to help break communication and leave you in control of the suit.

DEAL 44. DUCKING DANGER

```
                    ♠ K 7 5 2
                    ♥ K 8 7 4 3 2
                    ♦ J 2
                    ♣ 7

        ♠ Q 10 9                    ♠ A J 6
        ♥ J 6                       ♥ 5
        ♦ K 8 7 5                   ♦ 6 4 3
        ♣ J 9 3 2                   ♣ K Q 10 8 6 4

                    ♠ 8 4 3
                    ♥ A Q 10 9
                    ♦ A Q 10 9
                    ♣ A 5
```

South	West	North	East
1NT	P	2♣	Dbl
2♥	3♣	4♥	All Pass

Opening Lead: ♣ 2

Declarer won the opening lead and drew trumps. The contract needed a successful diamond finesse or a favorable spade position. Some days are just not your day. Down one.

Bad day? Unlucky as usual or was there a way home?

The danger is West leading a spade thru dummy's king. So leave East on lead at Trick 1; duck the opening lead! Say East returns a diamond. Now declarer is in control.

Win the diamond ace, draw trumps, cash the club ace discarding a diamond and start diamonds from hand, taking ruffing finesses, discarding spades.

It doesn't matter who has the diamond king. South loses two spades and one club, or one club, one diamond and one spade.

DEAL 45. NO WINNING OPTIONS

♠ 9
♥ A Q J 9 4 2
♦ J 10 9 8
♣ A 2

♠ 6 2   ♠ 5 43
♥ 7 5   ♥ K 10 8 6
♦ A Q 6 5 4   ♦ K 7 2
♣ Q 9 7 3   ♣ K J 10

♠ A K Q J 10 8 7
♥ 3
♦ 3
♣ 8 6 5 4

South dealt and opened 4♠.

West led the ♣ 3

Declarer starts with nine tricks. She knew if she tried to ruff a club by playing ace and a club, the defense would play a trump. She won the club ace, drew trumps, and took a heart finesse.

Down one.

The lead attacked the side-suit entry to the hearts. Any ideas?

The heart finesse is 50%. But try ducking the opening lead. What can the defense do? If a club is returned, win, then play the heart ace, then the heart queen which you plan to ruff. Now you can ruff a club, the tenth trick.

If instead East returns a trump, draw trumps, then start on the hearts either first the ace then the queen, or a finesse first. As long as the club ace is still in dummy, you are safe.

The defenders can't stop both a club ruff and heart establishment as long as you duck the first trick.

WHEN NOT TO DUCK

So now that we have learned all about ducking Trick 1, of course here come all the hands when it seems correct to duck and declarer should not duck. But that's what makes bridge what it is. It's not a game of set rules but of logic, of thinking out each problem.

So let's take a look at some examples when it seems correct to duck, and of course it is not.

DEAL 46. WIN OR DUCK?

♠ A 10 6
♥ 5 4 3
♦ K Q J 2
♣ Q J 10

♠ 9 3 2   ♠ Q J 7 5
♥ Q J 10 6 2   ♥ 9 8
♦ A 3   ♦ 8 7 5
♣ K 3 2   ♣ 9 7 6 4

♠ K 8 4
♥ A K 7
♦ 10 9 6 4
♣ A 8 5

South	West	North	East
1♦	1♥	2♥	P
2NT	P	3NT	All Pass

Opening Lead   ♥ Queen

Declarer ducked the first trick (maybe out of habit), and won the continuation. With only eight tricks, South knocked out the diamond ace, won the heart continuation and needing two club tricks took a club finesse. Down one.

Was there a better line of play?

With such a weak heart suit, chances were good West held the diamond ace & club king. Declarer should try for an endplay. To do this, he needs a throw-in card and the only card he can use is his low heart. So he must not duck Trick 1. If declarer wins Trick 1, knocks out the diamond ace, wins the heart continuation and cashes the diamonds and A-K of spades, what will West discard?

Declarer can then exit his preserved heart & after West cashes three heart tricks will have to lead from his club king to give declarer his ninth trick.

DEAL 47. MORE DANGEROUS TO DUCK

```
                    ♠ 7 2
                    ♥ Q 8 6
                    ♦ K Q 5 3
                    ♣ A K Q 2

    ♠ K Q 10 8 5 4                    ♠ 9 6
    ♥ J 10 7 4                        ♥ K 9 5 2
    ♦ A 9 6                           ♦ 8 7
    ♣ void                            ♣ 9 8 7 5 4

                    ♠ A J 3
                    ♥ A 3
                    ♦ J 10 4 2
                    ♣ J 10 6 3
```

West	North	East	South
1♠	Dbl	P	2NT
P	3NT	All Pass	

Opening Lead: ♠ K

Holding the A-J, it's usually right to hold up with the lead of the king. If West leads another spade, South scores two spade tricks. But East played the six, a low card so West switched to the jack of hearts. South played the queen, but when East produced the king, South had to cover and eventually lost one spade, one diamond, and three hearts for down one.

How could South have done better? What kind of hand is this?

It's a danger hand in more ways than one. Sometimes it's more dangerous to duck, especially when a shift can be dangerous. The one card South had to knock out, the diamond ace, was almost surely with West, the opening bidder, who could not attack spades if South won the opening lead and remained with the guarded J3.

After winning Trick 1 & knocking out the diamond ace, South has nine tricks.

DEAL 48. TAKE THE PLUS SCORE

♠ A Q 3
♥ K 4 2
♦ K 7 4 3
♣ 8 4 3

♠ 10 7 5 4   ♠ K 9 2
♥ 10 8 5   ♥ 9 7 6 3
♦ 8 5 2   ♦ A
♣ K 6 5   ♣ J 10 9 7 2

♠ J 8 6
♥ A Q J
♦ Q J 10 9 6
♣ A Q

South	North
1NT	3NT

Opening Lead: ♠ 4

Declarer, more out of habit, or perhaps it was match points, ducked the opening lead, a good chance that West had the king. East won and shifted to a club. This finesse lost, a club came back, and you know the rest of the story. Was it greed or was it carelessness?

How should declarer have played?

I don't know about you but if I bring back a card with all plus scores, or always make my contract, it's rare that I have a bad day.

Win the opening lead, give up a diamond, and now you are playing for overtricks if there are any. Nothing like a plus score.

Always ask "What could go wrong" and address the problem BEFORE, not AFTER it arises.

Do your thinking first.

DEAL 49. WIN AND HOPE

♠ A Q 5
♥ 7 2
♦ Q J 2
♣ A 6 5 4 3

♠ 9 6 4 2   ♠ 10 7 3
♥ J 10 6 5   ♥ A 9 8 4 3
♦ 3   ♦ A 6 5 4
♣ K Q J 10   ♣ 8

♠ K J 8
♥ K Q
♦ K 10 9 8 7
♣ 9 7 2

South opened 1♦ and North bid 2♣, game forcing. South bid 2NT and North bid 3NT. West led the ♣ King.

Declarer ducked the opening lead, again out of habit. West, seeing dummy, switched to a heart. South was soon down.

Could you have done better?

Having been fortunate to have not received a heart lead to start, declarer is still in danger if West has four clubs and an ace. So to prevent giving the defense a second chance to start hearts, win the opening lead.

As Hansel & Gretel said, "we are not out of the woods yet." But if West doesn't have an ace, you will make your contract.

DEAL 50. LOOKS RIGHT TO DUCK, BUT_____

♠ 4 3 2
♥ 9 7 6
♦ A J 6 2
♣ 9 5 4

♠ 10 5
♥ A Q 10
♦ K Q 9 8 7
♣ Q 7 6

♠ 9 6
♥ J 8 5 3 2
♦ 5 4
♣ 10 8 3 2

♠ A K Q J 8 7
♥ K 4
♦ 10 3
♣ A K J

South opened 2♣ and reached 4 ♠ after North raised spades. West led the ♦ King.

Declarer made the "book" play of ducking the opening lead, planning to take a diamond finesse later to discard a loser. West played another diamond and dummy's jack won. But when declarer played the diamond ace, East ruffed.

Having to now play out of his hand, he lost two hearts, one club, and one diamond. Down one.

Was there a successful line of play?

Forget the "book". Declarer must make the counter intuitive play of winning the first trick.

After drawing trumps, he can lead the diamond ten.

When West wins, whatever he plays back gives South his tenth trick.

DEAL 51. COMPRESSING NINE INTO EIGHT

♠ K J 5
♥ A K 8
♦ J 5 3
♣ A Q J 9

♠ 9 7 4 3
♥ 6 4
♦ 8 6 4 2
♣ 6 5 2

♠ Q 10 2
♥ Q 9 7 5 2
♦ A 9 7
♣ K 7

♠ A 8 6
♥ J 10 3
♦ K Q 10
♣ 10 8 4 3

North opened 1♣ and raised South's 1NT response to 3NT.

Opening Lead: ♥6

West led a heart, hoping to find his partner's suit. Declarer seeing at least three clubs and at least two in each of the other suits played low at Trick 1. West won and returned a heart.

Declarer came to his hand with the spade ace and took a losing club finesse. Back came another heart. Now with only seven tricks, declarer led a diamond. Down two.

Was there a road to nine tricks?

South should win the first heart, come to the spade ace and let the ♣10 ride. East can win the ♣K, but East has no winning options. A spade or heart costs a trick.

If East exits a club, declarer forces out the diamond ace and has at least nine tricks.

DEAL 52. ARE YOU A THINKING PLAYER OR A GREEDY PLAYER?

```
              ♠ AQ3
              ♥K42
              ♦K743
              ♣843

♠10754                    ♠K92
♥1085                     ♥9763
♦852                      ♦A
♣K65                      ♣ J10972

              ♠J86
              ♥AQJ
              ♦QJ1096
              ♣AQ
```

South opened 1NT and North raised to 3 NT. West led the ♠ 4.

Declarer had visions of a lot of tricks. If everything went well, maybe twelve tricks were possible. He played low at Trick 1. You know the "rest of the story".

East won the king and switched to a club. Twelve turned into eight.

What is the moral of this sad story?

When you are in a contract that seems laydown, always ask "What can go wrong?" It seems like it always does if you don't do your thinking before playing too quickly.

You are not playing matchpoints. Your goal is nine tricks, not twelve. Lock up those nine: ♠A, knock out the ♦A and you have your nine. If instead you play low and East has the ♠K, a club shift can establish the setting tricks before you get nine.

A thinking player would win the first trick. You can worry about the rest later.

DEAL 53. LISTEN TO THE BIDDING


```
              ♠ 8 7 3 2
              ♥ 4
              ♦ K Q 9 7 5 4
              ♣ Q 6

♠ Q 6                         ♠ K J 10 9
♥ K Q 10 9 7 5                ♥ 8 6 3
♦ A                           ♦ 8 3
♣ J 10 4 2                    ♣ 9 8 7 5

              ♠ A 5 4
              ♥ A J 2
              ♦ J 10 6 3
              ♣ A K 3
```

West	North	East	South
1♥	P	1♠	1NT
2♥	3NT	All Pass	

Opening Lead: ♥ King

Declarer had read a lot of books which said to duck and hope your LHO leads another heart, some kind of fancy-named coup. But West saw East's three and switched to the spade queen. East overtook with the king.

South had no winning option. If he took the ace, the defense would later run spades. If he ducked East would continue hearts. Ugh. He was sorry he had read that book.

What was the right play? Listen to the "book" or the bidding?

The problem is the ace of diamonds. If West has it, win the first trick; you have the guarded J2 of hearts. If East has it, you must duck. Missing sixteen HCP's, and East having a couple of points for a light response, West is a big favorite to have the diamond ace. Win Trick 1 and attack diamonds.

Five diamonds, two clubs, and two major suit aces. Don't give West a second chance to find the winning spade lead.

DEAL 54. GYPSY ROSE LEE

```
              ♠ A 4 3 2
              ♥ J 4 3 2
              ♦ A 8
              ♣ K Q 4

    ♠ 7 6                    ♠ 8 5
    ♥ A 10 9                 ♥ K 7 5
    ♦ J 9 4 3                ♦ K 10 7 6 5
    ♣ 10 8 6 5               ♣ 7 3 2

              ♠ K Q J 10 9
              ♥ Q 8 6
              ♦ Q 2
              ♣ A J 9
```

South opened 1♠ and North bid 2NT, a Jacoby Game Forcing raise with 4+ trumps. South bid 3NT, showing no shortness but not a minimum. North bid a conservative 4 ♠. West led the ♦ 3.

Declarer, looking at the diamond suit by itself, made the reflex play of ducking, hoping West had led from the king. East produced the king and returned the suit.

Later declarer had to tackle the heart suit himself and lost three tricks, down one. Could you have done better? What kind of deal is this?

Bridge is not an isolated trick but an entire deal. This is a Gypsy Rose Lee, a strip and throw-in so you don't have to lead hearts from your hand. So don't squander your throw-in card by ducking. South should win the diamond ace, draw trumps, eliminate the clubs, and exit a diamond.

The opponents have to start the hearts assuring South of a heart trick or offer a ruff/sluff, and South makes his contract.

DEAL 55. TIMING

♠ Q J 10
♥ A Q
♦ A 7 6 4 2
♣ 7 5 3

♠ 7 3   ♠ 5 4
♥ J 9 7 2   ♥ K 10 6 5 4
♦ K 10 8 5   ♦ J 9
♣ K 9 8   ♣ Q J 10 2

♠ A K 9 8 6 2
♥ 8 3
♦ Q 3
♣ A 6 4

North opened 1♦ and rebid 1NT after South's 1♠ response. South bid 4♠. West led the ♥ 2.

Declarer took the heart finesse at Trick 1. East won and shifted to the club queen. Declarer ducked this trick and won the second club as West unblocked his king. After drawing trumps, declarer exited a club and declarer had to lose a diamond.

How would you have played this hand?

As in all deals, hand pattern recognition is crucial. What kind of deal is this? A second suit and timing is important. Win the opening heart lead and play ace and another diamond, planning to set up the diamonds.

West wins, leads another heart to East who shifts to a club. But South is now in control.

He wins the ace and using trumps as entries can set up the fifth diamond for a club discard. Timing!

DEAL 56. WIN OR FINESSE?

```
              ♠ 3 2
              ♥ A Q 10 3
              ♦ J 2
              ♣ Q 9 4 3 2

  ♠ K 7 6                    ♠ Q J 10 9 8
  ♥ J 9 8 7 5                ♥ K 6
  ♦ 7 6 5                    ♦ A 10 9 8
  ♣ 10 6                     ♣ 8 7

              ♠ A 5 4
              ♥ 4 2
              ♦ K Q 4 3
              ♣ A K J 5
```

South opened 1NT and reached 3 NT after a Stayman auction. West led the ♥7.

This is the classic example of not seeing the forest. Declarer, after counting nine winners, couldn't resist a finesse, not seeing the danger.

East won the heart king and switched to a spade. Down two.

How should declarer have played?

If you like living on the edge, take the finesse. If you like making your contract, rise with the heart ace, and after losing a diamond you have nine tricks.

Not so bad. After all, think about those declarers who received a spade lead.

DEAL 57. TRY AGAIN; WIN OR FINESSE?

```
                    ♠ A Q 7 4
                    ♥ 9 2
                    ♦ A Q J 6 5
                    ♣ A Q

  ♠ 10 8 5 2                        ♠ K 9
  ♥ K 7 6                           ♥ Q 10 8 5 3
  ♦ 9 4                             ♦ 8 7 2
  ♣ J 9 8 6                         ♣ K 3 2

                    ♠ J 6 3
                    ♥ A J 4
                    ♦ K 10 3
                    ♣ 10 7 5 4
```

North opened 1♦ and raised South's 1NT response to 3 NT. West led the ♣6.

Declarer finessed the club queen. East won and returned the heart ten, jack, king. West returned the heart seven. The defense continued hearts, forcing out the ace.

When declarer's spade finesse lost, the defense cashed the rest of the hearts.

Was there a better line of play?

Declarer has nine tricks no matter how the clubs lie. He should win the club ace at Trick 1 and play a diamond to his hand.

After a losing spade finesse, the best the defense can do is take three clubs and one spade.

DEAL 58. ONCE MORE; WIN OR FINESSE?

          ♠ Q J 9 8 3
          ♥ J 5
          ♦ A J 3
          ♣ Q 10 6

♠ 5 2   ♠ A 7 6 4
♥ A K 10 2   ♥ 6 4 3
♦ 7 6 5 2   ♦ K 9 8
♣ 8 7 3   ♣ 9 4 2

          ♠ K 10
          ♥ Q 9 8 7
          ♦ Q 10 4
          ♣ A K J 5

South	West	North	East
1NT	P	2♥*	P
2♠	P	3NT	All Pass

• Transfer

Opening Lead: ♦ 7

Declarer instinctively played low, not foreseeing any danger. East won and seeing no future in diamonds reverted to the ♥6.. West won the king and returned the deuce.

The jack in dummy won but when South led a spade, the defense won and took two more hearts. Down one.

How should South take his nine tricks?

No finesses. Just grab the ace of diamonds at Trick 1 and force out the spade ace. He wins four spades, four clubs, and one diamond.

Bridge is an easy game.

DEAL 59. RISK-REWARD

♠ 10 5 3
♥ 8 6 5 4 2
♦ J 9 4
♣ A Q

♠ J 8 2
♥ Q 7
♦ K 7 2
♣ J 10 7 6 3

♠ Q 9 7 6 4
♥ J 10 9 3
♦ 8 5
♣ K 8

♠ A K
♥ A K
♦ A Q 10 6 3
♣ 9 5 4 2

South opened 2NT and North bid 3NT, treating his weak heart suit as a four card suit. West led the ♣6.

Missing two kings, declarer played dummy's queen, hoping for an overtrick. East won the king and returned a club. When the diamond king was offside, West cashed three more club tricks.

Down one, losing four clubs and one diamond.

Unlucky? Both kings offside, but declarer missed a sure play for the contract. Do you see it?

The contract was at risk if West held five clubs. But if West held ♣KJ1063, he might have led the jack.

If West had ♣K10863 and the diamond king, the contract was still safe.

The only way to go down was to finesse at Trick 1. By playing the ace, almost surely the suit would be blocked no matter which honor East held.

DEAL 60. BLOCK THEIR SUIT

```
                        ♠ Q 7 6
                        ♥ A Q 7
                        ♦ A 10 6 5 4
                        ♣ 9 2

        ♠ 4 2                           ♠ 9 5 3
        ♥ J 10 9 8 5 4                  ♥ K 3
        ♦ Q 3                           ♦ K J 9
        ♣ A 10 4                        ♣ 8 7 6 5 3

                        ♠ A K J 10 8
                        ♥ 6 2
                        ♦ 8 7 2
                        ♣ K Q J
```

West	North	East	South
2♥	P	P	2♠
P	4♠		All Pass

Opening Lead: ♥ Jack

At Trick 1, declarer took the heart finesse. East won the king. Declarer eventually lost one heart, two diamonds, and one club. Down one.

How should declarer play to make four spades?

You might start by asking what their lead agreements are. If (BIG if) you can get an answer, RHO will tell you jack denies a higher honor. In any case, play the ace at Trick 1; the queen can wait. Draw trumps ending in your hand and lead a heart.

If West plays the king, the queen provides a discard. If West plays low, just play low from dummy. Most likely East is down to a singleton king and again the queen is good for a discard.

62

DEAL 61. PLAYING BY HABIT

♠ 10 7 3
♥ Q 7
♦ 9 4 2
♣ A K 10 7 3

♠ K J 9 2
♥ 10 5 4 2
♦ K 6 5
♣ 6 4

♠ Q 6 4
♥ J 9 8
♦ Q 10 8 3
♣ Q 8 5

♠ A 8 5
♥ A K 6 3
♦ A J 7
♣ J 9 2

South opened 1NT and North bid 3NT. West led the ♠2.

East played the queen at Trick 1 & declarer ducked. East switched to the ten of diamonds, a surrounding play, covered by the jack and won by the king. West returned the six of diamonds to dummy's nine, East's queen and South won the ace. When declarer lost the club finesse, East cashed two diamonds for down one.

Was there a better line of play?

A hold-up play to break the opponent's communication is often a good play but not when there is the danger of a switch to a more dangerous suit.

Also the lead of the spade two is most likely from a four card suit.

So declarer should win Trick 1 & has nine tricks after losing a club finesse to East's queen.

DEAL 62. NO COUP FOR YOU

♠ 6 5 3
♥ K 8 2
♦ Q J 10 6 5
♣ 5 3

♠ Q 10 9 2   ♠ K J 8
♥ 10 5 3   ♥ 9 6 4
♦ K 4   ♦ 7 3 2
♣ K Q 10 6   ♣ 8 7 4 2

♠ A 7 4
♥ A Q J 7
♦ A 9 8
♣ A J 9

South opened 2NT and North raised to 3NT. West led the ♣King.

Declarer had read about the Bath Coup, holding up to encourage a continuation into his ♣AJ. But East had played the ♣2 at Trick 1, denying the jack.

West switched to the ♠2. Declarer ducked again but East returned a club. When West won the ♦K, he cashed two more club tricks.

Down one. "Partner," said North. "Not the time for your fancy Bath Coup."

Did you read the same book?

Sure, but there is a time and place for everything. This was not the time; it was more dangerous to duck.

As declarer, win Trick 1 since you still have the ♣J5. If the diamond finesse loses, it will be into the safe hand. West cannot attack clubs.

After losing to the diamond king, declarer has one spade, four hearts, four diamonds and one club.

Ten tricks. The Bath Coup can wait till the next time.

DEAL 63. THE WHOLE DEAL

```
                      ♠ 6 2
                      ♥ A 5
                      ♦ J 10 9 6 4
                      ♣ Q J 7 6

      ♠ K J 10 8 5              ♠ 9 7 4 3
      ♥ 7 4 2                   ♥ K J 10 9 3
      ♦ K 5                     ♦ 3 2
      ♣ 10 8 3                  ♣ 9 5

                      ♠ A Q
                      ♥ Q 8 6
                      ♦ A Q 8 7
                      ♣ A K 4 2
```

South   North
2NT   3NT
          All Pass

Opening Lead: ♥ 7

   Declarer, thinking the lead might be 4th best played low. What happened next was not pretty. East won the king and shifted to a spade. The finesse lost, back came another spade.

   When the diamond finesse lost, (of course), South finished down two.

   How would you play?

   I hope you wouldn't have let East, the danger hand, in so easily. Rise with dummy's ♥A at Trick 1 to keep him out, then lead dummy's ♦J to finesse into the safe hand. When it loses, you have an easy ten tricks.....eleven if West exits in either major.

   Don't duck out of habit. Look at the whole deal.

DEAL 64. SAME OLD PROBLEM

♠ J 7 5 4 2
♥ A Q
♦ Q 9 2
♣ J 6 4

♠ Q 8 3   ♠ 10 9 6
♥ J 10 7 6 4   ♥ K 8
♦ K 4   ♦ 7 5 3
♣ 10 8 2   ♣ Q 7 5 3

♠ A K
♥ 9 5 3 2
♦ A J 10 8 6
♣ A K

South opened 1♦ and rebid 2NT after North's 1♠ response. North simply bid 3 NT, rather than look for a 5-3 spade fit. West led the ♥6.

Declarer finessed at Trick 1, losing to East's king. East returned a heart. When the diamond finesse lost, declarer was down one. Unlucky or not well thought out?

How would you have played?

It's important to try to analyze the opening lead. South is in trouble only if West has a five card suit and a quick entry. But think about the lead. What would you lead from KJ108x or KJ10xx?

Almost for sure East has an honor and if doubleton, declarer can block the opponent's suit by playing the ace at Trick 1.

If East has Qx, West can only cash two tricks with KJ864 when he gets in. Declarer's nine is a big card.

66

DEAL 65. THINK FIRST

♠ A K Q 4 2
♥ 9 6 4 3
♦ 5 2
♣ K J

♠ 6 5
♥ Q J 10 8 7
♦ A 6 3
♣ 10 5 4

♠ J 10 9 7
♥ K 2
♦ 9 7 4
♣ Q 9 6 2

♠ 8 3
♥ A 5
♦ K Q J 10 8
♣ A 8 7 3

North	East	South	West
1♠	P	2♦	P
2♠	P	3NT	All Pass

Opening Lead: ♥Queen

East can't make the usual play of overtaking and returning since that would give declarer a second stopper. So he must play low. Declarer made the reflex play of ducking. Another heart went to the king and ace.

When West got in with the diamond ace, he cashed the hearts. Down one.

How should declarer have played?

The contract is cold if hearts are 4-3. If West has five to the QJ10xx, East has Kx.

So declarer can block the suit by winning Trick 1, seemingly contrary to most holdup principles.

East can't afford to unblock the king with the nine in dummy.

DEAL 66. SAVING WHAT YOU NEED

```
                    ♠ 7 6 3
                    ♥ J 10 5
                    ♦ A K 8 6
                    ♣ Q 4 2

    ♠ 10 4                          ♠ Q J 9 8 2
    ♥ 8 7 4 3 2                     ♥ A Q
    ♦ J 10 5 3                      ♦ 9 7
    ♣ 10 9                          ♣ K J 6 5

                    ♠ A K 5
                    ♥ K 9 6
                    ♦ Q 4 2
                    ♣ A 8 7 3
```

North	East	South	West
P	1♠	1NT	P
3NT		All Pass	

Opening Lead: ♠ 10

Declarer ducked the first spade and won the second spade. Knowing all the high cards were in the East hand, he led a diamond to dummy and led the heart jack. East won the ace & returned a spade.

Declarer took another heart finesse but ended with eight tricks, down one.

Was there a better line of play?

Ducking to break communication is usually a good technique but here holding up won't help for East has all the high cards.

If South wins the first trick and continues along the same line of play, he can later exit with the spade five. By holding up, declarer would squander his throw-in card.

After East takes his three good spades, he has only clubs & is endplayed into leading away from the king, giving declarer his ninth trick.

68

DEAL 67. TIMING; NO DUCKING, NO FINESSES

```
                    ♠ A K 10
                    ♥ 8 6 5 4 2
                    ♦ 8 6 2
                    ♣ A 3

        ♠ 7 3 2                      ♠ 6
        ♥ K 10 9 3                   ♥ Q J
        ♦ 10 7                       ♦ K Q J 5 4
        ♣ J 7 5 4                    ♣ K 9 8 6 2

                    ♠ Q J 9 8 5 4
                    ♥ A 7
                    ♦ A 9 3
                    ♣ Q 10
```

South opened 1♠. North showed a limit raise with three spades by first bidding 1NT forcing, then raising spades. South bid 4 ♠. West led the ♣4.

Facing four possible losers, declarer played low at Trick 1, taking the club finesse. East won and returned a diamond.

Possibility became reality. Down one.

Could declarer have found a better line of play?

Again it's hand pattern type recognition. Stop the finesses! This is a second suit type deal. Timing is crucial. Win the opening lead and get started on the hearts. Play the heart ace and another heart. The defense will win, cash a club and switch to a diamond but it's too late.

Declarer goes to dummy with a trump. When both opponents follow, the hand is cold. Ruff a heart, back to dummy with a spade, one more heart ruff and the last heart is good. The last spade is the entry to discard a diamond loser.

Ten tricks.

DECEPTION BY DECLARER

Entire books have been written on the art of falsecarding. These and other plays by a crafty declarer can often bring home an unmakeable contract by leading the defenders astray. Like a magician creating an illusion, declarer can make a hand seem like something other than it is.

Let's look at some examples of how at Trick 1, a clever declarer might pull the wool over his opponent's eyes.

DEAL 68. A DECEPTIVE DECLARER

```
                    ♠ 10 6
                    ♥ 4 3
                    ♦ Q J 7 2
                    ♣ J 10 9 8 5

                                        ♠ 2
                                        ♥ A 10 9 8 7 6 5 2
                                        ♦ A 10 9
                                        ♣ 2
```

East	South	West	North
4♥	6♠		
		All Pass	

Opening Lead: ♥ Queen

East won the ace at Trick 1, declarer following with the king. East tried to cash the diamond ace, declarer ruffed and claimed.

  Whose fault was this?

  Credit declarer with a good play. When the queen is led, East knows South has the king but the location of the jack is uncertain. From South's view, the king and jack are equals once the queen is led.

  A good principle is always get rid of the card you are known to hold.

  If South plays the jack at Trick 1, even the caddy knows to give West a ruff.

  The longer you hold on to known cards, the easier it is for the opponents to defend.

  Declarer's hand: ♠ A K Q J 9 8 5 3   ♥ K J   ♦ void ♣ A K Q

71

DEAL 69. AVOIDING A RUFF THRU DECEPTION

♠ J 3
♥ Q J 8 6 5
♦ Q 9 5
♣ K J 3

♠ A 10 9 7 6 542
♥ ----
♦ A J 10 2
♣ 4

South	West	North	East
1♥	P	3♥	4♠
6♥		All Pass	

Opening Lead: ♠ Q

East won the spade ace. Declarer made the slam when East tried to cash the diamond ace at trick two.

How did you do? Why did East not give West a ruff?

It depends what card South played at Trick 1. Did you play the king of spades under the ace, a card you are known to have? Sort of like a previous hand, no? If you let East think your spade was a singleton, you gave East something to think about. He might try to cash the ♦A before you could discard your singleton diamond on dummy's ♦J. South might have had a different hand like:

♠ K   ♥ A K 7 4 3 2 ♦ 7 ♣ A Q 10 9 6

But then he probably would have bid 4NT. East should infer South is void in diamonds and has falsecarded. East should find this inference. But it's worth a try. Not playing the king is giving up.

South's actual hand: ♠ K 8 ♥ A K 7 4 3 2 ♦ void ♣ A Q 10 9 6

DEAL 70. DECEPTION WHEN TROUBLE LURKS

```
                    ♠ 9 7
                    ♥ 7
                    ♦ Q 10 6 5 3
                    ♣ A K 10 3 2
      ♠ K J 5 2                    ♠ A 10 4 3
      ♥ Q 9 6 5 3                  ♥ 10 4
      ♦ A 7                        ♦ 9 8 2
      ♣ 9 8                        ♣ 7 6 5 4
                    ♠ Q 8 6
                    ♥ A K J 8 2
                    ♦ K J 4
                    ♣ Q J
```

South	North	
1NT	3♣^	^ Minors, Game Forcing, no slam interest
3♦*	3♥^	*Asks where is shortness, ^lower suit, heartshearts
3NT	All Pass	

Opening Lead: ♥ 5

North-South were playing 3♣ and 3♦ showed 5/5 in the minors, the latter being stronger. Declarer won the opening lead with the ♥J and not wanting to play clubs first and let the opponents signal, tried to slip the diamond king through for his ninth trick.

"Trying to catch me napping?" asked West rising with the ♦A.

Her ♠2 hit the table and four spade tricks defeated the contract.

Could you have caught a wide-awake West napping?

Perhaps, if you won Trick 1 with the ♥K. A nice bit of deception Mike Lawrence demonstrated recently is falsecarding at Trick 1 in a situation like this by winning with the king, not the jack. Then West might continue hearts to East's 'known' jack.

You don't need three heart tricks. If you win with the jack, West will know you have the AKJ and probably switch.

If you play the ace, both defenders will wonder why you didn't hold up; you probably have the king. Winning with the king is your best chance.

Kleinman's First Law of Falsecarding says declarer should falsecard with the lowest card that will do the job. Be credible as well as deceptive. A whisper speaks more convincingly than a shout.

DEAL 71. ANOTHER AVOIDING A RUFF

```
                    ♠ K 7 5
                    ♥ Q J 7 4
                    ♦ J 8 7 4
                    ♣ K 4

        ♠ 3                         ♠ A 9 8 6 4 2
        ♥ 9 6 2                     ♥ 8
        ♦ Q 10 9 6 5 3              ♦ A K
        ♣ J 10 6                    ♣ 9 8 5 2

                    ♠ Q J 10
                    ♥ A K 10 5 3
                    ♦ 2
                    ♣ A Q 7 3
```

South opened 1♥, North bid 3♥, a limit raise and South bid 4♥. West led the ♠3.

Play started five, ace, ten. Then the nine of spades (suit preference), spade ruff, diamond, spade ruff,

Down one. South shrugs & says "Bad luck".

Could declarer have done better?

Perhaps. South needed to at least put doubt into East's mind about the lead. Playing the ten was an error. East knows the missing cards are the QJ.

If West had QJ3, he would have led the queen. If South plays the queen, same story; West would have led the jack from J103.

But if South plays the jack at Trick 1, East might think West started with Q103 & now has a problem.

Hey, it never hurts to try.

DEAL 72. FALSECARD TO DISCOURAGE A SWITCH

```
                    ♠ 10 4 3
                    ♥ 7 5 4
                    ♦ K J
                    ♣ A J 9 8 3

        ♠ K J 6                      ♠ A 9 8 7 2
        ♥ J 10 9 6                   ♥ A 8 2
        ♦ 8 7 3                      ♦ 4 2
        ♣ 5 4 2                      ♣ Q 10 7

                    ♠ Q 5
                    ♥ K Q 3
                    ♦ A Q 10 9 6 5
                    ♣ K 6
```

South	West	North	East
1NT	P	3NT	All Pass

Opening Lead; ♥ Jack (Leading the jack denies a higher honor in their methods)

East won the ace of hearts, declarer playing the three, and from the opening lead knew the heart layout. East shifted to a low spade and South was soon down two.

Can South make 3NT after the same lead?

Take a mulligan and drop the heart queen under the ace, a known card. He would make 3NT if East continued hearts and go down with a spade switch. By creating the deception of starting with KQ doubleton of hearts, look what might happen. East may now read the opening lead as from ♥J10963 and continue hearts anyway.

East might think he would have time to get in and set up partner's heart suit.

A good play that couldn't cost but might gain.

DEAL 73. ANOTHER FALSECARD TO AVOID A SWITCH

North
♠ K 10 8
♥ 10 3
♦ 8 6 5 2
♣ K 10 9 5

East
♠ 7 5 4 3
♥ A 2
♦ K J 9 3
♣ 6 3 2

South opened 2NT and North bid 3NT. West led the ♥4 to East's ace, declarer playing the jack. East returned the ♥2.

Is this the right play? Why?

If your partner has led fourth best, how many hearts does she have? Right, four since you can see the ♥32.

So how many hearts does declarer have? Duh, right! Five!

So a more perceptive East will switch to a low diamond. The entire hand:

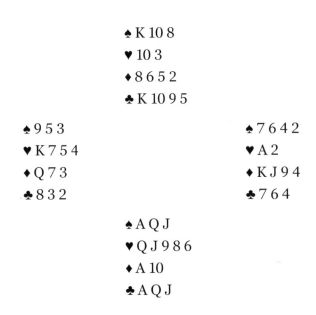

♠ K 10 8
♥ 10 3
♦ 8 6 5 2
♣ K 10 9 5

♠ 9 5 3   ♠ 7 6 4 2
♥ K 7 5 4   ♥ A 2
♦ Q 7 3   ♦ K J 9 4
♣ 8 3 2   ♣ 7 6 4

♠ A Q J
♥ Q J 9 8 6
♦ A 10
♣ A Q J

Opening 2NT with a five card major often has advantages by concealing a major part of your hand. I can't tell you how many times they lead your suit.

DEAL 74. MORE DECEPTION BY DECLARER

```
                    ♠ A 8 7
                    ♥ Q 8 4
                    ♦ K 6 5 4 2
                    ♣ Q 6

        ♠ J 3 2                      ♠ 5
        ♥ K J 5 3                    ♥ A 10 7 6
        ♦ 10 9                       ♦ Q J 7
        ♣ K J 9 2                    ♣ A 10 7 4 3

                    ♠ K Q 10 9 6 4
                    ♥ 9 2
                    ♦ A 8 3
                    ♣ 8 5
```

South	West	North	East
2♠	P	3♠	All Pass

Opening Lead: ♦ 10

Declarer won Trick 1 with the ace and drew trumps. Then he led a diamond and ducked in dummy, hoping the defenders might not cash their winners in the right order. South went down one.

Hopeless contract but with a little fancy footwork you might even make an overtrick. How?

Try ducking Trick 1, playing the eight from hand. This make's East's seven look encouraging so West might continue the suit. Win, draw trumps, making four!

Should the defenders fall for this? Why not? West may be suspicious, but looking at the two queens in dummy will not be too anxious to lead away from one of his kings.

Note that a thoughtful East might overtake the diamond ten at Trick 1 and switch.

DEAL 75. UNMAKEABLE BUT...

```
                    ♠ K 7
                    ♥ 10 9 7 5
                    ♦ K 9
                    ♣ A J 10 9 6

    ♠ 8 6 2                      ♠ Q J 9 5 3
    ♥ K 6 3                      ♥ 4
    ♦ J 8 7 6                    ♦ A Q 5 2
    ♣ 8 7 2                      ♣ K 5 3

                    ♠ A 10 4
                    ♥ A Q J 8 2
                    ♦ 10 4 3
                    ♣ Q 4
```

North	East	South	West
P	1♠	2♥	P
2♠	P	2NT	P
4♥		All Pass	

West led the ♠ 2. Declarer won in dummy and took a heart finesse. West won and shifted to a diamond.

East won two diamonds and later his club king.

Down one.

Was there any successful road to four hearts?

Not really, but as often happens never give up. You might try the effect of winning the opening spade lead in hand to lead a low trump. West will likely play low and dummy will win. Now play a trump to your ace and lose the club finesse.

East will lead back a spade, but declarer can discard two diamonds before West ruffs in.

Making four hearts, losing one heart, one club, and one diamond.

DEAL 76. AVOIDING A RUFF

```
                        ♠ Q 8 3
                        ♥ Q 8 6 5 3
                        ♦ K
                        ♣ 8 7 6 4

        ♠ J 10 2                        ♠ 7
        ♥ 7                             ♥ A K 10 9 2
        ♦ 10 8 7 6 3                    ♦ A 9 5 2
        ♣ J 10 9 2                      ♣ Q 5 3

                        ♠ A K 9 6 5 4
                        ♥ J 4
                        ♦ Q J 4
                        ♣ A K
```

East	South	West	North
1♥	1♠	P	2♠
P	4♠	All Pass	

Opening Lead: ♥ 7

East cashed the A-K of hearts & played a third heart. When West turned up with the J102 of trumps, South was down one.

Just bad luck or could South have played differently?

Hard to say but South could make a better effort at Trick 1 by playing the jack of hearts.

Now East has to consider if West is leading from 74 doubleton.

Instead of playing a second top heart, East might decide a club switch is better.

Playing a higher spot card than the card led in these situations may create doubt.

Why not, what do you have to lose?

DEAL 77. MORE OF THE SAME

```
              ♠ K 8 7
              ♥ A J 10 8
              ♦ K 5
              ♣ 9 5 4 3

  ♠ A                        ♠ 6 4 2
  ♥ 9 4 2                    ♥ K 7 6 3
  ♦ A 7 6 2                  ♦ J 10 9 8 3
  ♣ Q 8 7 6 2                ♣ 10

              ♠ Q J 10 9 5 3
              ♥ Q 5
              ♦ Q 4
              ♣ A K J
```

North-South reached 4♠ after South opened 1♠ and North showed a three-card limit raise.

West led the ♣6.

Declarer won the opening lead with the jack and led a trump. West won and led the club deuce, suit preference for diamonds. East ruffed, returned a diamond and ruffed another club.

Down one.

How would you play the hand to make the contract with the same opening lead?

At Trick 1, try the effect of winning the opening lead with the ace, a card you are known to have, creating the illusion of not having the jack.

When West wins the spade ace, there will be no thought of a club ruff.

South will eventually throw the club jack on the high heart in dummy.

DEAL 78. DECEPTION TO CREATE AN ENTRY

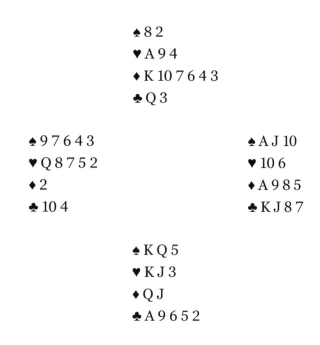

♠ 8 2
♥ A 9 4
♦ K 10 7 6 4 3
♣ Q 3

♠ 9 7 6 4 3
♥ Q 8 7 5 2
♦ 2
♣ 10 4

♠ A J 10
♥ 10 6
♦ A 9 8 5
♣ K J 8 7

♠ K Q 5
♥ K J 3
♦ Q J
♣ A 9 6 5 2

East	South	West	North
1♣	1NT	P	3NT

Opening Lead: ♥ 5

The first trick went heart five, four, ten, jack. Declarer played two rounds of diamonds; when West showed out, he could not overtake. East certainly has the club king. Declarer needs an extra entry. Do you see it?

Certainly West has the heart queen; East would have played it, not the ten. So declarer can lead towards the A9. But West can foil this by playing the queen. No more second entry, no 3NT.

Was there a better line of play?

At Trick 1, declarer should have won the king, not the jack. Now when you lead towards the A9, West "knows" East has the jack & is unlikely to play the queen.

You have your second entry, making 3NT. Very nice!

DEAL 79. DECLARER SIGNALS TO THE DEFENDERS

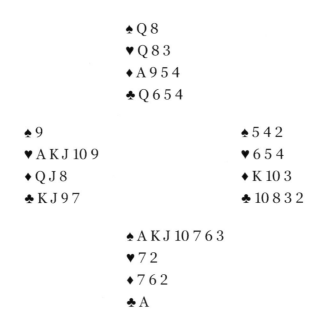

```
                    ♠ Q 8
                    ♥ Q 8 3
                    ♦ A 9 5 4
                    ♣ Q 6 5 4

        ♠ 9                         ♠ 5 4 2
        ♥ A K J 10 9                ♥ 6 5 4
        ♦ Q J 8                     ♦ K 10 3
        ♣ K J 9 7                   ♣ 10 8 3 2

                    ♠ A K J 10 7 6 3
                    ♥ 7 2
                    ♦ 7 6 2
                    ♣ A
```

West	North	East	South
1♥	P	P	2♠
P	3♠	P	4♠

Opening Lead: ♥ Ace

2♠ in the pass-out seat showed a good hand, long strong spades with seven or eight playing tricks. Weak jump overcalls are only in the direct seat. North may have bid 2NT or 3NT over South's 2♠. When you hold three queens, strain to play in notrump. The first trick went three, four, two. Seeing East's card West switched to a diamond and South was quickly down one.

Was this inevitable or could declarer have played differently?

A good rule in bridge is declarer can "signal" to a defender if declarer wants a suit continued or prefers a switch. If declarer had played the seven at Trick 1, West might think East had a doubleton and continued hearts, setting up the heart queen for a diamond discard.

A general rule is declarer should signal like a defender; high if you want the suit continued, low if you prefer a switch. The opposite is true if the defenders are playing "upside-down."

This often will cause the defenders to misread their partners carding.

DEAL 80.   DECLARER TELLS DEFENDERS WHAT TO DO

♠ Q J 3
♥ Q J 8 7
♦ K 8 7 3
♣ A 8

♠ A K 10 8 4
♥ 3
♦ A 9
♣ Q 9 6 5 3

♠ 7 6 5
♥ 10 9
♦ 10 6 5 2
♣ K 10 4 2

♠ 9 2
♥ A K 6 5 4 2
♦ Q J 4
♣ J 7

North	East	South	West
1♦	P	1♥	1♠
2♥	P	4♥	All Pass

Opening Lead: ♠Ace

The first trick went ace, three, five, two. Seeing the spots, West shifted to a club and South was soon down one.

Just another case of bad luck/overbidding or could South have tried to improve his chances?

Again, South should "signal" West by playing the nine at Trick 1.

This will at least create a losing option if West believes West might have started with 5-2 doubleton and is looking for a ruff.

Nothing ventured, nothing gained. Remember, a high card by declarer when you want the defender to continue the suit.

Try to become a more annoying declarer.

DEAL 81. MORE SIGNALING TO THE DEFENDERS

```
                    ♠ K J 7 4
                    ♥ Q 5
                    ♦ Q 8 3
                    ♣ K Q J 10

      ♠ 9 6                          ♠ 2
      ♥ A 3                          ♥ J 9 8 7 6
      ♦ 10 7 5                       ♦ A K J 4
      ♣ 9 8 6 4 3 2                  ♣ A 7 5

                    ♠ A Q 10 8 5 3
                    ♥ K 10 4 2
                    ♦ 9 6 2
                    ♣ void
```

East	South	West	North
1♥	1♠	P	2♥
P	2♠	P	4♠

All Pass

Opening Lead: ♥ Ace

The first trick went ace, five, six, two. East's card looked discouraging so West switched to a diamond and South was quickly down (again). Maybe he better not keep bidding so much?

As usual, there was a way to improve his chances. How?

South should play the ten at Trick 1, concealing the low cards.

If West thinks East is encouraging in hearts and continues, South is home via a marked ruffing finesse in clubs.

Again, declarer should signal an encouraging card to the defender.

- Note East's pass at his second turn. A good agreement to have in this situation is when you open, LHO overcalls, and RHO cue bids your suit, double says do NOT lead my suit. Pass means it's OK to lead your suit which is probably what partner was going to do. Here East certainly does not want a heart lead. West may have to guess, clubs or diamonds, but at least it's better.

DEAL 82. WHICH CARD TO FALSECARD?

```
                    ♠ A K J 4
                    ♥ Q 7 4
                    ♦ A K
                    ♣ K J 7 4

        ♠ 5                          ♠ Q 8
        ♥ A K 10 8 6 5               ♥ 3
        ♦ Q 3 2                      ♦ 10 9 6 5 4
        ♣ A 10 5                     ♣ Q 9 8 6 3

                    ♠ 10 9 7 6 3 2
                    ♥ J 9 2
                    ♦ J 8 7
                    ♣ 2
```

West	North	East	South
1♥	Dbl	P	1♠
2♥	3♠	P	4♠
	All Pass		

Opening Lead: ♥ Ace

South certainly suspects East has a singleton heart. If West continues hearts, South is going down. So South played the jack at Trick 1 hoping to make West think declarer has the singleton.

West continues hearts, giving East a ruff, down one.

How did West know and what should South have done?

As discussed, declarer should signal in the same way defender would. The two would say stop. Why? If South plays the jack, West knows the missing cards are the nine and two. Why would East play the 3 from 932 ?

If South plays the nine, same thing. The three from J32 ?

No, so the best play is the two. Then you have a chance.

DEAL 83. DECEPTION BY DECLARER

```
                    ♠ J 10 2
                    ♥ 9 5 3
                    ♦ 8 7 4 2
                    ♣ A 4 3

        ♠ 9 6 3                      ♠ 8 7 5 4
        ♥ Q 8                        ♥ J 10 7 4 2
        ♦ K J 9 3                    ♦ A 10 5
        ♣ J 10 9 8                   ♣ 7

                    ♠ A K Q
                    ♥ A K 6
                    ♦ Q 6
                    ♣ K Q 6 5 2
```

South	West	North	East
2♣	P	2♦	P
2NT	P	3NT	All Pass

Opening Lead: ♣ J

South won the opening lead and continued clubs. When West won the fourth club he shifted to a diamond after East had discouraged in hearts and spades.

Down one, the eight tricks South started with.

Was there a ninth trick?

Maybe. West's lead looks to be from a four-card suit. Declarer can only hope it's not from five. Try playing low from dummy at Trick 1 and the club six from hand, letting the club jack win the first trick. But it's important to prepare to play the ♣6 before playing low from dummy so that you can duck smoothly, not having to sit and be thinking when it's your turn to play. Be prepared to falsecard.

West naturally will continue clubs, East's seven looking encouraging and you have nine tricks.

"CHEAP" TRICKS

Often at Trick 1 declarer has an opportunity to win a "cheap" trick, with a lower card than necessary. Is this free gift in his/hers best interests? Maybe, maybe not. This is one time to count the gift **horse's teeth,** for a variety of reasons.

On the next series of hands, let's examine some cheap tricks or free gifts and see what to do with them; take them or reject them and why.

DEAL 84. NO FREE FINESSE; SAVE YOUR ENTRY

```
                        ♠ Q 4
                        ♥ K J 10
                        ♦ 7 2
                        ♣ A K J 8 6 3

        ♠ 7 6 3                          ♠ 8 5
        ♥ Q 8 5 3 2                      ♥ 9 7 6
        ♦ A Q 2                          ♦ 10 9 8 4
        ♣ 7 5                            ♣ Q 10 9 2

                        ♠ A K J 10 9 2
                        ♥ A 4
                        ♦ K J 6 5
                        ♣ 4
```

South opened 1♠ and after North bid 2♣, game forcing. North-South bid easily to 6♠.

West led the ♥3.

The 10 of hearts won the first trick. South drew trumps, cashed the heart ace and discarded a diamond on the A-K of clubs.

When the club queen didn't fall, declarer tried to guess the diamonds and went down.

Could South have done better?

What kind of deal is this? Yes, a second suit which means preservation of entries. Instead of taking the free finesse at Trick 1, South must overtake the "winning" ♥10 with the ace of hearts to preserve an entry.

Cash the club ace, ruff a club, spade ace, spade to the queen, ruff another club.

Draw the last trump, and the preserved heart king is the entry to the good clubs to discard diamonds.

By the way, would you declare any differently at matchpoints? An overtrick would turn a good board into a cold top. Expecting others to bid and make 6♠, I'd go all out at matchpoints for seven and finesse dummy's ♥J on the second round.

DEAL 85. DANGER HAND; NO FREE FINESSE

```
                    ♠ Q 2
                    ♥ K J 6 5
                    ♦ Q 9 6
                    ♣ Q 10 8 4

     ♠ A J 9 7 3                    ♠ 8 5
     ♥ A 9 2                        ♥ 8 7 4
     ♦ 10 7 4                       ♦ J 8 5 3 2
     ♣ A 6                          ♣ 7 5 2

                    ♠ K 10 6 4
                    ♥ Q 10 3
                    ♦ A K
                    ♣ K J 9 3
```

West	North	East	South
1♠	P	P	Dbl
P	2♥	P	2NT
P	3NT	All Pass	

Opening Lead: ♠ 7

South played low from dummy at Trick 1, accepting the free finesse, winning the ♠10. South led a club; West played the ace, then the A-J of spades. South won but had only eight tricks: two spades, three diamonds, three clubs. South led a heart, West won and cashed two more spades for down one.

How should South have played?

All the high cards are marked with West, the danger hand, With three aces to lose, declarer can drive out the aces of hearts and clubs to get three tricks in those suits along with three top diamonds. South does not need more than one spade trick. What he needs from spades are stoppers. By letting the opening lead come around to his hand, South kills one of his stoppers.

South should play the spade queen at Trick 1. When West wins the club ace, there is no winning defense. Another spade lead gives South an extra spade trick and time to set up the hearts. Whatever West does, he gets only the three aces.

DEAL 86. GIVE UP A "FREE" TRICK

♠ Q J 10
♥ A J 8 3
♦ Q
♣ A 10 6 4 3

♠ 9 7 5 4 3   ♠ K 8
♥ K 9 2   ♥ 10 7 6 5
♦ 7 3   ♦ A 5 4 2
♣ K 9 5   ♣ J 8 7

♠ A 6 2
♥ Q 4
♦ K J 10 9 8 6
♣ Q 2

North opened 1♣ and rebid 1♥ after South responded 1♦. South bid 3NT.

West led the ♠7.

East covered the queen with the king giving declarer three spade tricks. Declarer then started the diamonds by leading the king. When East did take the diamond ace, he led back a spade.

Now declarer had three spades, five diamonds, and two side aces. Ten tricks but one problem. He was in the dummy and is still there today.

Which hand are you in?

Declarer only needs two spade tricks, but he needs transportation. If he lets East win the first trick, preserving his only sure entry to his hand, he will score two spades, five diamonds, and two side aces.

DEAL 87. DUCK A GIFT; PLAY SLOWER

```
                  ♠ A 7 4
                  ♥ K Q J
                  ♦ 8 6 4
                  ♣ 7 6 4 3

     ♠ K                         ♠ J 9 8 3 2
     ♥ 8 7 5 3                   ♥ 9
     ♦ K J 9 7 3 2               ♦ Q 10
     ♣ K J                       ♣ Q 10 8 5 2

                  ♠ Q 10 6 5
                  ♥ A 10 6 4 2
                  ♦ A 5
                  ♣ A 9
```

West	North	East	South
1♦	P	1♠	2♥
P	3♥	P	4♥

Opening Lead: ♠ K

West opened a marginal 1♦ with his 6-card suit, perhaps just a tad too strong for 2♦. South fell in love with his aces and bid game after North's raise. Everyone overbidding a bit.

Declarer quickly won the opening lead, a gift(?) and cashed the K-Q of trumps. When East showed out, South played much slower but had to lose four tricks. If he led a spade to his 10 at Trick 4, West would ruff and the defense would still get a diamond, a club, and a spade.

How should South have played? Do you remember this hand from the chapter on ducking?

He doesn't gain a fourth spade trick by winning Trick 1. He can finesse against the jack later. He need let the king of spades hold the first trick to preserve the dummy entry he will need to take that finesse after drawing trumps and West shows out in spades. If West shifts to a trump, declarer can draw trump, go to the spade ace & lead a spade to the 10, winning 5 trump tricks, 3 spades, and 2 minor aces.

DEAL 88. AVOIDING A GUESS

```
                    ♠ Q J 3
                    ♥ Q J 10 9
                    ♦ A 8
                    ♣ K 10 9 7

      ♠ X 8 7 4                      ♠ X 5
      ♥ X 7 6 5 2                    ♥ X
      ♦ K 2                          ♦ J 10 9 6 5 4
      ♣ 5 4                          ♣ Q J 8 2

                    ♠ K 10 6 2
                    ♥ K 8 3
                    ♦ Q 7 3
                    ♣ A 6 3
```

North	East	South	West
1♣	2♦	Dbl*	P
2♥	P	2NT	P
3NT		All Pass	

• Negative Double

Opening Lead: ♦ King

Declarer won the opening lead, a free trick. He now had to decide which major to start. East certainly didn't have both major aces. He randomly picked one which turned out to be the one West had the ace.

West continued diamonds. When East got in with the other major ace, he ran the rest of the diamonds.

Unlucky? If he started the other major first, he would have made 3NT.

Instead of having to guess, declarer should simply duck Trick 1.

West can continue with his second diamond but now South can start either major and succeed.

DEAL 89. THANKS, BUT NO THANKS

                          ♠ K 9 3
                          ♥ 4 2
                          ♦ 8 5
                          ♣ K Q J 10 7 6

        ♠ Q 10 7 6 4   ♠ 8 5 2
        ♥ A 6 3   ♥ K 10 9
        ♦ J 10 7 3   ♦ Q 9 6 2
        ♣ 9   ♣ A 8 3

                          ♠ A J
                          ♥ Q J 8 7 5
                          ♦ A K 4
                          ♣ 5 4 2

South choose to open 1NT instead of 1♥. North bid 3NT. West led the ♠6.

The first trick went three, eight, jack. Declarer, counting on plenty of tricks, started the clubs but when East held up until the third round, declarer realized he had no entry to the dummy.

The clubs are still sitting there as you read this.

How should declarer have played?

This is the classic example of "no thanks' at Trick 1. Turn down the free gift of the jack. It's too valuable as an entry to the clubs to take it now. Win the ace and later the jack is the entry to the clubs.

Taking nine tricks instead of seven.

DEAL 90. WINNING TOO CHEAP

```
                  ♠ 4 3
                  ♥ 6 3 2
                  ♦ K 7 5 3 2
                  ♣ J 10 3

    ♠ J 8 5                      ♠ Q 10 9 7
    ♥ J 9 4                      ♥ K Q 8 7
    ♦ 9 8 4                      ♦ J 10 6
    ♣ Q 9 8 4                    ♣ 7 5

                  ♠ A K 6 2
                  ♥ A 10 5
                  ♦ A Q
                  ♣ A K 6 2
```

South opened 2♣ and North bid 2♦, waiting. South bid 2♥ which this pair played as a Kokish relay, forcing North to bid 2♠. South's subsequent 2NT bid was forcing and North bid 3NT.

West led the ♣4.

South played the club jack at Trick 1 which won the trick. Declarer then cashed the A-Q of diamonds. When South led a low club, West rose with the queen and returned a club.

South ended with eight tricks, down one.

Was there a better line of play?

South was too anxious to win the first trick as cheaply as possible. By winning the first trick in hand, declarer is sure of an entry to dummy, having two little clubs and thanks to the 3/3 division of the diamonds has eleven tricks.

DEAL 91. FORCING AN ENTRY; DON'T WIN CHEAPLY

```
                    ♠ 4 2
                    ♥ 9 4
                    ♦ Q 6 4
                    ♣ Q J 10 6 5 2

    ♠ Q 10 8 7                    ♠ A 9 5
    ♥ 8 5 2                       ♥ Q 10 7 6 3
    ♦ K 10 8 3 2                  ♦ 9 7
    ♣ 4                           ♣ K 8 7

                    ♠ K J 6 3
                    ♥ A K J
                    ♦ A J 5
                    ♣ A 9 3
```

South opened 2NT and North bid 3NT. West led the ♦3.

 East played the nine and South won the diamond jack and led the club three. The defense ducked the first two club tricks. Declarer could take a successful finesse in a major suit but would end up with three clubs, two diamonds, and either three hearts or two hearts and one spade.

 South couldn't get back to the good clubs. If he led a low diamond, West would win, blocking the suit. If he led the jack, West would duck.

 How could South have done better?

 At Trick 1, South should ask himself "From what holdings might West have led the ♦3?" Answer: Unless West has made an implausible choice to lead from ♦1083 with more appealing major suit leads available, West has the ♦K.

 By winning the first trick with the ace, rather than cheaply with the jack, South is assured of a later entry to dummy's good clubs.

DEAL 92. A FREE TRICK CONVERTS TEN TO NINE

♠ A 5 3 2
♥ Q J 10 4
♦ 8 3
♣ 10 7 5

♠ 9
♥ 9 8 3
♦ A 9 5 4 2
♣ K 9 3 2

♠ 7 4
♥ K 7 6 2
♦ Q J 10 7
♣ Q J 6

♠ K Q J 10 8 6
♥ A 5
♦ K 6
♣ A 8 4

When North raised South's opening 1♠ bid to 2♠, South bid 4♠. West led the ♥9.

Declarer, happy that the opening lead was not a club, put up dummy's queen of hearts and East declined to cover.

Since the diamond ace was offside, declarer was limited to nine tricks: six spades, two hearts, and one club.

Since ten tricks were available, how should South have played?

The "free" trick at Trick 1 was an illusion.

If South takes the ace at trick one, with proper play he has six spades, the club ace, and can't be prevented from taking three heart tricks after giving up the king. Of course declarer has to take care to draw trumps only with honors from his hand, preserving dummy's ♠A as the entry to the hearts.

DEAL 93. A FREE GIFT COSTS AN ENTRY

```
              ♠ K Q 10 9
              ♥ J 2
              ♦ J 7 5
              ♣ A K 4 2

    ♠ 4 3                      ♠ J 8 7 5
    ♥ A 6                      ♥ 8 7 5 3
    ♦ A 8 4 2                  ♦ Q 10 3
    ♣ Q 10 8 7 3               ♣ 9 6

              ♠ A 6 2
              ♥ K Q 10 9 4
              ♦ K 9 5
              ♣ J 5
```

North opened 1♣ and South bid 1♥. When North bid 1♠, South bid 3NT. West led the ♠4.

South saw lots of tricks. She played the nine, insuring four spade tricks. East covered with the jack, South the ace.

South now led a heart to the jack, winning and another heart to her king and West's ace. West played another spade.

South now has four hearts, four spades & two clubs. But having them & getting them are not the same. With no sure entry to her hand, South ended with one heart, four spades and two clubs. Down two.

"Where did your tricks go," asked North?

South needed to win the first trick in dummy to preserve her only sure entry to the hearts. She was in 3NT, not 4NT.

Trying for ten when you need nine and ending up with seven is falling prey to greed.

DEAL 94. ANOTHER FREE GIFT, ANOTHER LOST ENTRY

```
                    ♠ K J 7 6 3
                    ♥ Q 7 3
                    ♦ 4 3
                    ♣ J 4 2

    ♠ 4                            ♠ 10 9 8 5 2
    ♥ A 10 8 6 4                   ♥ 5 2
    ♦ Q 9 2                        ♦ J 10 8 5
    ♣ Q 10 6 5                     ♣ K 7

                    ♠ A Q
                    ♥ K J 9
                    ♦ A K 7 6
                    ♣ A 9 8 3
```

South opened 2NT. North transferred to spades and bid 3NT. West led the ♥6.

The first trick went 6, 3, 5, 9. Declarer saw she needed at least four spade tricks. She led the ace & queen, but West showed out on the second spade.

Since overtaking was no longer an option, declarer needed to find an entry to dummy.

That queen of hearts looks nice, but declarer can't get there. If she leads the jack, West will play the ace, blocking the suit. If she leads the king, West will duck. Say good-bye to the spade suit.

How should South have played?

If one uses the Rule of Eleven, declarer should realize East has no card higher than the six.

So the queen is a sure entry for later as long as declarer saves the heart nine and wins the first trick with the king, assuring a later entry.

DEAL 95. NO THANKS; OVERTAKE, OVERTAKE

      ♠ 6 3
      ♥ 9 3 2
      ♦ Q 10
      ♣ K J 10 9 8 3

♠ Q 2   ♠ K J 10 7
♥ K J 10   ♥ 7 6 4
♦ J 9 8 6 5 3   ♦ 7 4
♣ 5 2   ♣ A 7 6 4

      ♠ A 9 8 5 4
      ♥ A Q 8 5
      ♦ A K 2
      ♣ Q

At favorable vulnerability, North violated his own oath to preempt only on jack high and opened 3♣. South bid 3NT.

West led the ♦6. "Got some extras for you, partner," he said, putting down the dummy.

Declarer won the opening lead in dummy, the ten being high. But it was all downhill from there.

Declarer played the club king but that was the end of the clubs and the end of 3NT. "That will teach me to preempt at favorable with extras," mumbled North.

How should declarer have played?

Overtake and overtake, first in the diamond suit at Trick 1, saving the two, another overtake of the club at Trick 2.

But if you fail the first test, the second part is moot.

DEAL 96. AVOIDING THE FREE FINESSE

♠ 8 2
♥ Q J 5
♦ A K Q 6
♣ J 9 4 3

♠ 9 7 3   ♠ 6 5 4
♥ 10 9 8   ♥ K 7 4 3
♦ 9 5 4 3   ♦ 10 8 7 2
♣ K Q 2   ♣ 6 5

♠ A K Q J 10
♥ A 6 2
♦ J
♣ A 10 8 7

After a 1♠ opening, a game-forcing 2♦ response and a 3♣ "high reverse," South bulldozed his way to slam, placing the contract in 6♠. West led the ♥10.

Declarer played the heart queen, taking the opportunity for a free finesse. East played low. Declarer drew trumps but could not untangle the diamonds and reach dummy.

Only eleven tricks.

Where did declarer go wrong?

Declarer must win the first trick with the ace, not take the "free" finesse.

Then he can draw trumps, unblock the diamond jack and can't be prevented from reaching dummy with a heart.

DEAL 97. SAVING YOUR ENTRY

♠ Q 10 9
♥ 7 6 5 4
♦ 8
♣ Q J 10 8 3

♠ A J 7 5 3   ♠ 8 2
♥ J 8 2   ♥ Q 10 9 3
♦ K 9 2   ♦ A Q 5 3
♣ 5 4   ♣ A 7 2

♠ K 6 4
♥ A K
♦ J 10 7 6 4
♣ K 9 6

South opened 1♦ and rebid 1NT after North's 1♥ bid. West led the ♠5.

Dummy plays the nine, East plays the eight to show count, and declarer the four. Declarer needs to find seven tricks. Clubs is the obvious source but East holds up till the third round. And now declarer starts thinking about how to get to dummy.

It's a little late to be doing your thinking.

If you still have the king of spades in your hand, you won't get to dummy unless the defenders put you there. And unless you are playing against your cousins, that's unlikely. No 1NT for you.

How should declarer have played?

In dire need of an outside dummy entry should the ♣A be guarded more that once, declarer needs to preserve both his low spades to forge a spade entry to dummy later.

Using the Rule of Eleven, East should not have a card higher than the eight. Just win Trick 1 with the king.

This gives you a near guarantee for making an overtrick rather than down one. Your choice.

Notice if you swap the East-West hands, 1NT is a hopeless contract. 3♣ is the right spot. Do you have the proper methods to reach and stop in 3♣?

DEAL 98. NO FREE FINESSE; SAVE YOUR ENTRY

♠ 7 2
♥ Q J 10
♦ A J 10 9 8 4
♣ 8 3

♠ Q 6 3   ♠ J 10 8 5
♥ 9 7 6 4   ♥ K 5 3
♦ 7 3   ♦ K 5 2
♣ Q 7 5 2   ♣ A 6 4

♠ A K 9 4
♥ A 8 2
♦ Q 6
♣ K J 10 9

South opened 1NT and North bid 3NT. West led the ♥7.

Declarer played dummy's ten at Trick 1, East played low as did South. Declarer came to his hand with a spade and took a diamond finesse. East ducked once, won the second and exited a spade.

Declarer had no entry to the dummy. Ace and a heart would lose, and if declarer led a low heart East can win, the suit being blocked.

How could this have been avoided?

Declarer was careless at Trick 1. (A nice way to say greedy). If declarer wins the ace at Trick 1, he has a sure later dummy entry to use the diamonds.

Here is a similar layout. Dummy has Q109 and declarer AJ8. In a similar situation, declarer would need to win the ace at Trick 1 to be able to force his way back to dummy later if necessary.

DEAL 99. AVOID BLOCKING THE SUIT

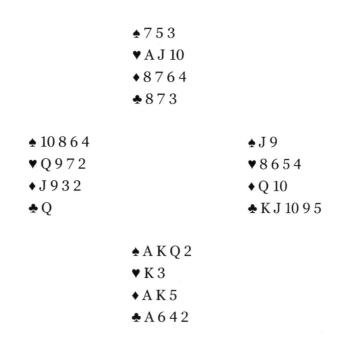

```
              ♠ 7 5 3
              ♥ A J 10
              ♦ 8 7 6 4
              ♣ 8 7 3

  ♠ 10 8 6 4                    ♠ J 9
  ♥ Q 9 7 2                     ♥ 8 6 5 4
  ♦ J 9 3 2                     ♦ Q 10
  ♣ Q                           ♣ K J 10 9 5

              ♠ A K Q 2
              ♥ K 3
              ♦ A K 5
              ♣ A 6 4 2
```

South opened 2NT and North bid 3NT. West led the ♥2.

Declarer played dummy's ten which won the trick. Then to try to find a ninth trick tested the diamonds but they were 4-2, and ended with eight tricks, down one.

How would you have played 3 NT?

Declarer went down at Trick 1 by not playing the heart king on the ten. Then later he can take a heart finesse if necessary. After winning the heart king at Trick 1, declarer can cash the ♠AK; if both follow then the ♠Q. If spades are 3-3, he is home. If not, the ♦AK; if both follow, another diamond.

Declarer still has the heart finesse as a last resort. West was likely to have the queen, both from the opening lead and East's play to Trick 1. Another unnecessary gift resulting in a laydown contract failing.

A LITTLE OF THIS, A LITTLE OF THAT

And of course there are some hands that don't fall into any of the previous chapters but should be included in any book on the subject of playing to Trick 1.

Here is a small collection of interesting problems.

DEAL 100. FINESSE OR NOT?

♠ 10 9 3
♥ A J 6 2
♦ 9 7 6 3 2
♣ Q

♠ K 4 2   ♠ 6 5
♥ 7 5   ♥ Q 10 9 8 3
♦ A 10 8 5   ♦ K J
♣ J 9 6 3   ♣ K 10 8 4

♠ A Q J 8 7
♥ K 4
♦ Q 4
♣ A 7 5 2

South opened 1♠ and North bid 2♠. South made a game try, bidding 3♣. North was unsure and made a 'counter game try', bidding 3♥. South bid 4♠. West led the ♥7.

At Trick 1, declarer finessed the jack, hoping to set up a discard for a losing diamond. It went heart jack, queen, king. Now declarer played ace of clubs and ruffed a club.

South then cashed the heart ace and ruffed a heart. West overruffed and returned a trump.

With only one trump left in dummy, South ended losing two diamonds and two clubs. Down one.

Was there a better line of play?

Once declarer had received a favorable lead, not a trump or diamond, she had to watch her entries to ruff three clubs. Win Trick 1 in dummy with the heart ace.

Now club ace, club ruff, heart king, club ruff, and heart ruff with the spade ace.

She can ruff the last club in dummy and has three more trump tricks in hand. Ten tricks in all.

DEAL 101. PRESERVING YOUR ENTRIES

♠ A Q 2
♥ A J 10 9
♦ A K
♣ 8 6 4 3

♠ J 9 7 6 4
♥ 8 3 2
♦ 8 5
♣ A K J

♠ 10 8
♥ K 7 6
♦ 10 9 7 6 3 2
♣ 7 2

♠ K 5 3
♥ Q 5 4
♦ Q J 4
♣ Q 10 9 5

North opened 1♣ and raised South's 1NT response to 3NT. West led the ♠6.

Declarer, looking at three or four heart tricks, and six tricks in spades and diamonds, and clubs well guarded, forgot to ask "what can go wrong?" She won the opening lead in hand to lead the heart queen for a finesse.

East won and continued spades. Unfortunately for declarer, after cashing the A-K of diamonds, she was never able to get back to her hand to cash the diamond queen.

Lots of tricks suddenly became only eight, down one.

"What happened to your tricks," asked North?

Do you see the answer?

Declarer was in 3NT, not 4NT. She only needs three heart tricks so she should win the opening lead in dummy. By starting the hearts from the top, she might sacrifice one trick but assures three spades, three hearts, and now three diamonds.

The carefully preserved spade king is the entry to the diamond queen.

DEAL 102. GETTING OUT OF YOUR OWN WAY

♠ J 10 9
♥ K 6 3
♦ A J 5 2
♣ 8 6 4

♠ Q 7 6 5 2   ♠ A 4
♥ Q 10 9   ♥ 8 7 5 2
♦ 10 6 3   ♦ K Q 9
♣ 7 2   ♣ K 9 5 3

♠ K 8 3
♥ A J 4
♦ 8 7 4
♣ A Q J 10

South	North
1NT	2NT

Opening Lead: ♠ 5

East won the spade ace and returned the four. Declarer's plan was to try to bring in the clubs for four tricks. He played a heart to dummy's king and took a successful club finesse. He then went to dummy's diamond ace and repeated the club finesse.

With no other entry, he played the club ace but the king did not drop. Down one for lack of another entry.

Unlucky? Could you have found another entry?

Yes. At Trick 1 declarer must unblock his spade king under the ace. This doesn't cost a trick and creates a third entry to bring in the clubs for four tricks.

107

DEAL 103. JUST LIKE THE LAST ONE

                    ♠ A 7 2
                    ♥ J 10 9
                    ♦ 4 2
                    ♣ J 9 4 3 2

    ♠ Q 9 8 3   ♠ J 6 5 4
    ♥ Q 6 5 4 3   ♥ A 2
    ♦ 9 7   ♦ K 8 5
    ♣ A 10   ♣ K 8 7 5

                    ♠ K 10
                    ♥ K 8 7
                    ♦ A Q J 10 6 3
                    ♣ Q 6

Playing on-line, at IMP scored pairs, South misclicked and opened 2NT. North bid 3NT.

West led the ♥4.

Declarer needs one heart, two spades, and six diamonds tricks. East won the opening lead and returned the suit.

With only one entry to dummy, declarer played a spade to the ace and took a diamond finesse to the ten. When the king didn't fall next under the ace, the contract failed.

Could you have found the extra entry needed to repeat the finesse?

Like the previous hand, just unblock the heart king under the ace, the same as you should with Qxx.

Now you can repeat the diamond finesse and pick up the needed six diamond tricks.

DEAL 104. HOGGING THE NOTRUMP?
BETTER PLAY BETTER

♠ A Q 8 3
♥ A Q 2
♦ J 10 4 2
♣ J 4

♠ 9 6 2   ♠ K J 10 7
♥ 10 9 8 4   ♥ K 6 3
♦ Q 7 6   ♦ K 9 8 3
♣ K 8 5   ♣ 7 3

♠ 5 4
♥ J 7 5
♦ A 5
♣ A Q 10 9 6 2

South opened his shapely but minimal strength hand 1♣ and North bid 1♥. Instead of a normal 2♣ rebid, South grabbed the hand by rebidding 1NT to protect his hearts against an opening lead thru them, as he later explained to his partner. North raised to 3NT but looking at his hand wondered who should be declarer. West led the ♥10. "See why I was right to bid notrumps first?" South gloated when he saw dummy. "If the lead is from ♥K109, it's only from my side we can get three heart tricks."

Declarer played low from dummy. East won the king and shifted to a low diamond; four, queen, two. The diamond return took away the last entry from declarer's hand. He went to dummy with a heart and led the club jack.

West ducked but won the second club. Declarer never got his long clubs and went down three.

"Partner," said North, "If you are going to grab them, you better make them."

How would you have made 3NT if you had grabbed it?

Declarer needed one more entry. Play the heart queen from dummy at Trick 1. If East wins the ♥K, he cannot dislodge both of declarer's two outside entries to the club suit. If East ducks, declarer starts clubs from dummy at Trick 2 and still has the ♦A as an entry to run the rest of the clubs after West wins the ♣K.

DEAL 105. SETTING UP A FINESSE POSITION

♠ Q 7 5 2
♥ A 10 4
♦ 9 7
♣ 8 6 4 3

♠ A 3   ♠ 8 6
♥ Q 9 8 6   ♥ K 7 5 3
♦ 8 6 4 3 2   ♦ K Q 10 5
♣ K 2   ♣ 9 7 5

♠ K J 10 9 4
♥ J 2
♦ A J
♣ A Q 10

South opened 1♠ and North raised to 2♠. South made a game try, bidding 3♣ and North bid 4♠. West led the ♥6.

Declarer played low from dummy. East won the king and returned the king of diamonds. South won the ace, drew trumps, went to dummy and took a club finesse. Down one.

How would you play the hand?

The real question is not "What do you play?" but "What DID you play?" After losing to the heart king, you could take a heart finesse to get rid of your diamond loser. But (BIG but) only if you discarded the heart jack under the king at Trick 1.

This leaves you with a small heart opposite the A10 in dummy, not the jack opposite A10. Now if West has the queen of hearts, likely from the play at Trick 1, East's king, you are making four spades.

DEAL 106. TOO MANY FINESSES

♠ 8 6 4
♥ A J 7 4
♦ K J 5
♣ 4 3 2

♠ A Q 3
♥ K Q 10 8 5 3
♦ 9
♣ K 6 5

♠ J 7 5 2
♥ 9 6 2
♦ Q
♣ J 10 9 8 7

♠ K 10 9
♥ void
♦ A 10 8 7 6 4 3 2
♣ A Q

South opened 1♦ and West overcalled 1♥. When North bid 1NT, South bid what he thought he could make- 5♦. West led the ♥K.

Declarer won the ace, discarding a spade. He cashed the diamond king and took a club finesse, losing to West's king. West returned a club.

Declarer crossed to dummy with a trump to lead a spade to his king. West won the ♠AQ. Down one.

"Partner," moaned North. "Didn't you read Dr J's book 'The Finesse, Only A Last Resort'?"

How would you have played this contract?

The discard on the heart ace can wait since declarer really doesn't know what he wants to discard. Ruff the opening lead keeping the ♥AJ in dummy. Then cross to the ♦K and lead a spade covering East's card.

West will win and is endplayed in three suits. If he leads a heart or club, he gives declarer a free finesse. If he cashes a high spade, declarer's spade is high and he will discard the club queen on the heart ace.

One finesse is fine, but that's enough.

Making five diamonds.

DEAL 107. I'M ALWAYS IN MY OWN WAY

♠ 8 2
♥ Q 7 6 4
♦ 6
♣ A K 8 6 4 3

♠ A Q 9 4
♥ 10
♦ Q 10 7 3
♣ Q J 10 5

♠ J 7 6 3
♥ J 9 8 3 2
♦ 9 5 4
♣ 7

♠ K 10 2
♥ A K 5
♦ A K J 8 2
♣ 9 2

South opened 1♦ and rebid 2NT after North responded 1♥. North raised to 3NT. West led the ♣Q.

Declarer decided not to duck since a spade shift might be dangerous. Setting up the long clubs seemed best so South won the ace, East playing the seven, and came to his hand with a spade.

His plan was to lead a club.

If West plays an honor he planned to cover and continue with the eight, forcing out the last high club. But West did not cover. The nine won but with only one entry, declarer could not use the club suit.

Did you do any better?

Did you remember to unblock the club nine at Trick 1? Now you are leading the two and if West plays low from J105 you can finesse the eight.

Then it's easy to set up the clubs and you have the heart entry.

DEAL 108. UNBLOCKING

♠ J 8 4
♥ 9 7 6
♦ Q 6 2
♣ K J 10 4

♠ 6 5   ♠ K 10 7 2
♥ K 4 3   ♥ A Q 5 2
♦ A 10 8 7 5   ♦ 9 4
♣ A 8 6   ♣ 9 7 5

♠ A Q 9 3
♥ J 10 8
♦ K J 3
♣ Q 3 2

South opened 1♣. What should North bid? 1NT? Raise clubs? A standard 1NT response after 1♣ should show a good hand, 8 – 10 HCP. North had no desire to be the declarer with this hand and made the proper bid of 1♦. South rebid 1NT. Bidding 1♠ should imply an unbalanced hand with at least four clubs.

West led the ♦7. East played the nine and declarer won the jack without much thought. When he started on the club suit, East gave count so West knew to win the third round. West switched to the heart three. East won and led another diamond.

Declarer was toast. Holding ♦K3 opposite dummy's ♦Q6, he had no way to reach dummy. If he played the king, West would duck. If he played low, West would win and the suit was blocked. With no way to take the spade finesse, he was down one.

The solution?

Mike Lawrence always said that some innocent plays can turn out to haunt you in the strangest ways.

At Trick 1, win with the king, not the jack and the defenders could not prevent you from reaching dummy's diamond queen and fourth club. Seven tricks: Two spades, two diamonds, and three clubs.

DEAL 109. TAKE YOUR TIME

                    ♠ 8 5 2
                    ♥ J 10 4
                    ♦ K 6 5
                    ♣ 7 6 4 2

    ♠ K J 9 7 4   ♠ 6
    ♥ 9 3   ♥ K 8 7 6 5
    ♦ 9 7 4   ♦ A 8 3
    ♣ K 5 3   ♣ J 10 9 8

                    ♠ A Q 10 3
                    ♥ A Q 2
                    ♦ Q J 10 2
                    ♣ A Q

South opened 2NT and North raised to 3NT. West led the ♠7.

North tabled the dummy, "thank you" said South, "two please". East followed and declarer won the ten. South played the diamond queen which won, then a diamond to the king and East's ace.

Back came the club jack, queen, king. Unable to get to dummy for a heart finesse, declarer finished with eight tricks.

Question: What do you think of South's play?

Much too fast. Remember, think BEFORE Trick 1, not after. If South had done that and used the Rule of Eleven, he would realize the eight of spades in dummy at Trick 1 was the proper play.

Now with the heart finesse available, declare can score two spades, three hearts, three diamonds and one club.

Nine beats eight any day.

DEAL 110. TAKE YOUR TIME AGAIN

                          ♠ A J 3
                          ♥ A 9 4 3 2
                          ♦ Q J 8
                          ♣ A Q

      ♠ 9 7 6 5   ♠ Q 8 2
      ♥ K 10   ♥ Q J 7 5
      ♦ 6 5 4   ♦ A K 10 9
      ♣ 10 8 5 2   ♣ 6 3

                          ♠ K 10 4
                          ♥ 8 6
                          ♦ 7 3 2
                          ♣ K J 9 7 4

North opened 1♥ and South bid 1NT, which they played as forcing for one round. When North bid 2NT showing 18-19 HCP, South bid 3NT. West led the ♠7.

Declarer played low from dummy and won East's queen with his king. He continued with a club to the ace and overtook dummy's club queen with his king. When East discarded on the third round of clubs, declarer could only take eight tricks. Down one.

Unlucky or in too much of a hurry?

Too much of a hurry. If you think about it at Trick 1, you'll play dummy's jack, ensuring a spade entry to your clubs later. If the ♠J holds, your ♠K remains an entry. If East covers with the ♠Q, your ♠10 becomes an entry.

As an extra precaution. after East covers and you win the ♠K, you can lead towards dummy's diamonds at Trick 2 to give yourself an extra chance: a diamond trick in case clubs provide only four tricks.

Thanks to Tim Bourke, IBPA, of Canberra for this theme.

DEAL 111. PLEASE PARTNER, JUST
MAKE YOUR CONTRACT

♠ K 5 4
♥ J 7
♦ 5 4
♣ Q J 10 9 7 6

♠ Q J 10 7 3   ♠ 9 8
♥ 9 8 6   ♥ Q 10 4 2
♦ A 8   ♦ 10 9 7 6 3 2
♣ K 5 2   ♣ 8

♠ A 6 2
♥ A K 5 3
♦ K Q J
♣ A 4 3

South	North
2NT	3NT

Opening Lead: ♠ Queen

Declarer won the king in dummy and led the club queen. Everyone followed low and South said "Guess we missed a slam, partner." North cringed, having seen and heard this before. On the next club East showed out.

South now showed that twelve potential tricks do not always equal nine real ones. South ended with eight tricks, two in each suit.

Do you think North is calling South for another game?

How would you have played 3NT?

With only one sure dummy entry, win Trick 1 in hand and start the clubs by playing ace and another. South will score two spades, two hearts, five clubs and even if you get no diamonds you make your game.

DEAL 112. WATCH THOSE SPOTS

♠ A Q J 10 3
♥ void
♦ K Q 10
♣ K J 9 8 7

♠ K 5 4
♥ A J 9 8 7 6 4
♦ 5 3
♣ 2

♠ void
♥ 5 3 2
♦ A 9 8 4 2
♣ 10 6 5 4 3

♠ 9 8 7 6 2
♥ K Q 10
♦ J 7 6
♣ A Q

South opened 1♠ and West bid 3♥, preemptive. North cue bid 4♥, knowing South would sign off in 4♠, then bid 4NT. This shows a heart void and tells partner not to count the ace of that suit. Why?

If North had a 4NT bid, why did he not bid it over 3♥? Nothing happened to encourage him. This is a form of "Exclusion." North-South reached 6♠. West led the ♥A.

Declarer ruffed the opening lead low in dummy. He had a sure diamond loser but if he could pick up the spade suit, six spades was making. He played a club to his ace and took a successful spade finesse. But East showed out.

OK, so declarer came back to the club queen to take another finesse. West ruffed the diamond. Ouch, not OK. Now a diamond to East and another club ruff. Down two. Definitely not OK since the hand was cold for twelve tricks.

How should South have made the slam?

With a little forethought. If declarer ruffs with the spade queen at Trick 1 and comes to hand, he can lead the spade nine and win the first finesse in hand, not the dummy.

Now a second spade finesse picks up the spade suit without having to go back and forth.

DEAL 113. WATCH THOSE TRUMP SPOTS

♠ K J 6 2
♥ A Q 9 6 3
♦ Q 6 5
♣ 5

♠ 9 8 4   ♠ 7
♥ 8 2   ♥ K J 10 5 4
♦ A 3 2   ♦ K J 9 4
♣ K 10 8 7 3   ♣ J 6 2

♠ A Q 10 5 3
♥ 7
♦ 10 8 7
♣ A Q 9 4

South opened 1♠ and North bid 4♣, which they played as a forcing spade raise showing either a singleton club or a void and at least four spades. With either 2 or 6 of his HCP possible worthless, South retreated to 4♠ to discourage a slam. West led a small trump, the ♠4.

Declarer played the two from dummy. the seven from East and won in hand. He started a crossruff; ace of clubs, club ruff, ace of hearts, heart ruff, club ruff.

He ruffed another heart with his five but West overruffed with the eight and led his last trump.

Declarer still had four more losers.

How would you have managed your way to ten tricks?

The question to ask yourself at Trick 1 is, "Which suit can I least afford to ruff low twice, hearts or clubs?"

With eight clubs in the defender's hands but only seven hearts, you can least afford to ruff hearts low twice.

So keep only one low trump in the hand that will ruff hearts and two low trumps in the hand that will ruff clubs.

This means winning Trick 1 with one of dummy's honors and crossruffing from there. Now ruff two clubs with dummy's low trumps and one heart with the five of trumps, crossruff with high trumps and take ten tricks.

DEAL 114. SAFETY PLAY

        ♠ A J 10 9 4
        ♥ 6 5 3
        ♦ K 6 3 2
        ♣ 5

♠ K 6 2   ♠ Q 8 7 5
♥ A Q J 10 7   ♥ 9 8
♦ J 10 9 4   ♦ 8 7 5
♣ 8   ♣ J 9 4 2

        ♠ 3
        ♥ K 4 2
        ♦ A Q
        ♣ A K Q 10 7 6 3

South	West	North	East
1♣	1♥	1♠	P
3NT		All Pass	

Opening Lead: ♦ Jack

Declarer won the first two diamond tricks in hand, went to the spade ace, cashed the diamond king, and started the clubs, getting ready to claim eleven tricks. When West showed out on the second club, South was down more than he could count.

Can you make 3NT against most layouts?

You need to protect against a 4-1 club break. If West has four clubs he can't hurt you. You have nine tricks. But if East gets in, a heart play thru your king will be fatal.

So how do you get to dummy to take a club finesse? Certainly not with a spade as that would create a spade entry to East, the danger hand. So just win the first trick with the diamond king and finesse the club ten.

Win or lose, your contract is assured.

DEAL 115. WHERE TO WIN THE FIRST TRICK?

```
                    ♠ K Q 5 3
                    ♥ K 4
                    ♦ A Q J
                    ♣ Q J 7 3

    ♠ A 6 4                      ♠ 9 8 7
    ♥ Q J 10 8 7                 ♥ 6 5 2
    ♦ 9 6                        ♦ 10 8 7 3
    ♣ A K 5                      ♣ 9 8 2

                    ♠ J 10 2
                    ♥ A 9 3
                    ♦ K 5 4 2
                    ♣ 10 6 4
```

West	North	East	South
1♥	Dbl	P	1NT
P	3NT	All	Pass

Opening Lead: ♥ Queen

Declarer won the heart king in dummy and cashed the A-Q-J of diamonds. He played a spade to his jack, West played low. Declarer cashed the diamond king and led another spade. West ducked again.

West won the third spade and played the heart jack. Declarer could not reach the high spade in dummy and had only eight tricks.

How does the deal play if declarer wins Trick 1 in hand?

He can play to dummy's three high diamonds and come back to his hand with a spade. West can duck but declarer cashes the high diamond and forces out the ace of spades. He wins the next heart in dummy and cashes the good spade for the ninth trick.

Not easy to see at Trick 1 without playing the whole deal in your mind before playing to Trick 1.

DEAL 116. WHERE TO WIN THIS ONE?

```
                    ♠ Q J 7 4
                    ♥ A 7 6 3
                    ♦ A 8 3
                    ♣ 5 3

        ♠ A 3                        ♠ 8 6
        ♥ J 10 9 8 4                 ♥ Q
        ♦ Q J 2                      ♦ 10 7 6 5 4
        ♣ K Q 2                      ♣ J 10 8 7 6

                    ♠ K 10 9 5 2
                    ♥ K 5 2
                    ♦ K 9
                    ♣ A 9 4
```

West	North	East	South
1♥	P	P	1♠
P	2♥	P	4♠

Opening Lead: ♥ Jack

It looks pretty routine, three losers, one in each suit except diamonds. Declarer played low out of habit (or fear of an unlikely ruff?) and won the king. When he led a trump, West won the ace and led another heart. This time South's fears were realized. He now had an extra loser and was down one.

Could this have been avoided?

East is not ruffing Trick 1. With the lead of the jack, it's almost a certainty East has a singleton queen. So declarer should win the ace in dummy to keep declarer's ♥K from getting ruffed on the second heart lead.

Now the play continues the same but when West leads another heart, if East ruffs, he is ruffing a loser, not one of your winners.

121

DEAL 117. VERY SHORT SECOND SUIT; TIMING

                    ♠ K 5 3
                    ♥ 9 7 4 2
                    ♦ Q J 6
                    ♣ J 7 4

    ♠ Q J 10 8   ♠ 9 7 2
    ♥ A K   ♥ 6
    ♦ 9 7 4 2   ♦ A 10 8 5
    ♣ 9 8 5   ♣ Q 10 6 3 2

                    ♠ A 6 4
                    ♥ Q J 10 8 5 3
                    ♦ K 3
                    ♣ A K

South reached 4♥ after a 1♥ opening and a simple raise. West led the ♠Q.

Declarer won in dummy and led a heart. West's ♥K won and he continued the ♠10 to drive out dummy's ♠K. East won the ♦A next. The ♠9 was the setting trick.

Down one.

"Partner, at least make a little effort please," begged North.

What did North mean?

Declarer can make a little effort. Fast losers, OK, nowhere to go. But let's try to avoid the slow loser, in this case the spade with better timing. Win Trick 1 in hand preserving dummy's ♠K, in case the defenders duck the first diamond. Then the ♦K and another diamond if the first diamond wins. Win the spade return in dummy and discard your last spade on dummy's high diamond.

Now it's time to draw trumps. Making four hearts.

DEAL 118. POSTPONING A DISCARD

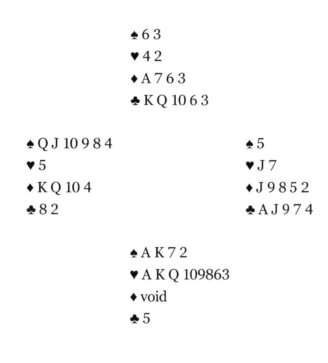

```
                          ♠ 6 3
                          ♥ 4 2
                          ♦ A 7 6 3
                          ♣ K Q 10 6 3

     ♠ Q J 10 9 8 4                      ♠ 5
     ♥ 5                                 ♥ J 7
     ♦ K Q 10 4                          ♦ J 9 8 5 2
     ♣ 8 2                               ♣ A J 9 7 4

                          ♠ A K 7 2
                          ♥ A K Q 109863
                          ♦ void
                          ♣ 5
```

South	West	North	East
2♣	3♠	4♣	P
4♥	P	5♦	P
6♥		All Pass	

West, at favorable vulnerability, jammed the auction with his weak but shapely 6-4 hand with good spot cards. South wasn't sure what North's bids meant so he bid what he thought he could make. East's failure to double for a club lead led West to lead the ♦K.

Declarer was in a hurry; he took dummy's ace to discard his club loser. Then he drew trumps and more trumps but nothing good happened. West clung to his spades and took two tricks at the end.

Declarer was in such a hurry. Given East's kindness, could you have made this ridiculous slam?

There is no rush to discard the club. Count winners as well as losers. Ten tricks in hand plus a club and diamond from dummy if you can set up a club. So preserve dummy's ♦A as a possible entry. Ruff the opening lead and draw trumps. Cash the top spades and play East for the ♣A. With only clubs and diamonds remaining, East will have to put you in the dummy. Twelve tricks, thank you.

DEAL 119. IMPROVING YOUR CHANCES

                          ♠ Q J 10 3
                          ♥ void
                          ♦ J 10 9 7 6
                          ♣ Q J 10 7

        ♠ 2   ♠ K 8 7 5 4
        ♥ K Q J 9 8 7 4 2   ♥ 10 6 5 3
        ♦ 3   ♦ K 2
        ♣ K 8 2   ♣ A 3

                          ♠ A 9 6
                          ♥ A
                          ♦ A Q 8 5 4
                          ♣ 9 6 5 4

South	West	North	East
1♦	4♥	5♦	All Pass

Opening Lead: ♥ King

Declarer won the heart ace. With two club losers he played the ace of diamonds hoping to drop a singleton king, then get to dummy for a spade finesse.

Down one.

Was there a better plan?

Declarer was going to need luck in spades and diamonds but missing three to the king, the odds favor taking a finesse.

Lead the diamond jack for a finesse.

What wrong hand? Didn't you ruff the heart ace at Trick 1 ?

DEAL 120. RULE OF ELEVEN

This deal occurred in a team game scored at IMP's The auction was the same in both rooms.

```
                        ♠ K Q J 10 9
                        ♥ Q 8 4
                        ♦ 8 7 4
                        ♣ 8 2

        ♠ A 7 3                        ♠ 8 6 5 4 2
        ♥ A J 9 6 2                    ♥ 7
        ♦ J                            ♦ K 9 6 5 2
        ♣ Q 10 9 4                     ♣ 7 6

                        ♠ void
                        ♥ K 10 5 3
                        ♦ A Q 10 3
                        ♣ A K J 5 3
```

South	West	North	East
1♣	1♥	1♠	P
2♦	P	2♠	P
2NT	P	3NT	All Pass

In one room, West led the ♥6. Declarer had caught up on her reading since the last hand. Using the Rule of Eleven, she played dummy's ♥8 which won the trick. Then she led the spade king and discarded the ♣3.

When West saw declarer discard, he wanted to tear up his cards after his opening lead. With the ♥Q as an entry, declarer had plenty of tricks.

And in the other room?

After a similar auction, West led a club. This gave declarer an extra club trick, but the spades are still sitting there as you read this.

Perhaps it's best to follow Mike Lawrence's good advice on these types of hands. When your partner shows a weak hand and you have a void in his suit, it's usually best to pass and let him play in his suit.

DEAL 121. A SCARY MOMENT OR A SAFE ONE?

♠ J 4
♥ Q 5 3 2
♦ Q 9 3
♣ Q J 6 3

♠ A K 10 7 5 2   ♠ 6 3
♥ 6 4   ♥ A 10 9 8 7
♦ 2   ♦ K 7 5
♣ 10 7 4 2   ♣ 9 8 5

♠ Q 9 8
♥ K J
♦ A J 10 8 6 4
♣ A K

West	North	East	South
2♠	P	P	3NT

Opening Lead: ♠ 7

Declarer played low to assure a spade trick and East followed with the six. With no entry to dummy, he tried the diamond ace hoping the king was singleton. Nope. Hand over, down, down, down. Maybe a little overbid?

Any ideas how declarer might do better?

This hand is from Mike Lawrence who points out that no matter how many books you read, things come up at the table that require thought. If you use the Rule of Eleven and the bidding, you might have played the jack from dummy at Trick 1, the winning play.

A scary moment but logical. Now the diamond finesse. If East covers the queen, you have eleven tricks. Thanks Mike.

DEAL 122. GIVE UP A SURE WINNER?

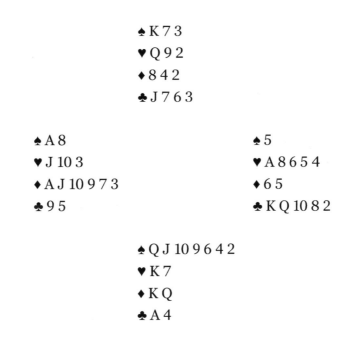

```
              ♠ K 7 3
              ♥ Q 9 2
              ♦ 8 4 2
              ♣ J 7 6 3

  ♠ A 8                        ♠ 5
  ♥ J 10 3                     ♥ A 8 6 5 4
  ♦ A J 10 9 7 3               ♦ 6 5
  ♣ 9 5                        ♣ K Q 10 8 2

              ♠ Q J 10 9 6 4 2
              ♥ K 7
              ♦ K Q
              ♣ A 4
```

South	West	North	East
1♠	2♦	2♠	Dbl*
4♠		All Pass	

• Clubs and hearts

Opening Lead: ♥ Jack

East won the heart ace and shifted to the club king. Declarer saw a potential loser in each suit but a possible discard on the heart queen. He won the club ace, cashed the heart king and led a low spade hoping to get to dummy. But West went up with the spade ace and the defense cashed their two minor winners. Down one

Unlucky? Overbid? Or what would you have done?

Unless declarer was playing against a relative, his line of play was hopeless. But if he had discarded the heart king under the ace, he could have led the seven towards the Q9 in dummy, playing West for the ten. Now he has a discard for his club loser. If East ducks the first trick, none of the above happens. West wins the first trump & shifts to a club setting up three defensive tricks. If South leads a heart, the nine forces the ace but declarer has no third heart.

DEAL 123. WHO NEEDS THAT KING?

                    ♠ A J 7 6 2
                    ♥ 10 3
                    ♦ Q 6 2
                    ♣ J 7 2

    ♠ 9 8   ♠ Q 10 5 4 3
    ♥ 6 5   ♥ K 8
    ♦ 10 8 5 3   ♦ A J 4
    ♣ Q 9 6 5 3   ♣ K 10 8

                    ♠ K
                    ♥ A Q J 9 7 4 2
                    ♦ K 9 7
                    ♣ A 4

East	South	West	North
1♠	Dbl	P	1NT
P	2♥	P	2NT
P	4♥	All Pass	

Opening Lead: ♠ 9

Declarer played low, then tried to reach dummy with a diamond to take a heart finesse, He must have been in the men's room during the bidding, losing two diamonds, one heart, and one club.

Down one.

If you listened to the bidding, how would you have played?

All the missing high cards on with East. You can afford to lose two diamonds and one club.

Win the spade ace at Trick 1, (who needs that king) and take a successful heart finesse.

128

DEAL 124. FINESSES CAN WAIT

♠ J 9 5 3
♥ A J
♦ A J 7
♣ J 9 8 7

♠ A Q 2
♥ 7 6
♦ 10 9 6 4 2
♣ A K 2

♠ 10 6 4
♥ 9 8 5 4 2
♦ Q 3
♣ 6 4 3

♠ K 8 7
♥ K Q 10 3
♦ K 8 5
♣ Q 10 5

South opened 1♣ and North bid 1♠. South rebid 1NT and North bid 3NT. West led the ♦4.

Declarer played the jack and East played the queen. Whether declarer ducked or won, 3NT was doomed. The defense could set up the diamonds before declarer could set up a ninth trick in spades.

What should declarer have played at Trick 1?

There was no rush to take the finesse; it wasn't going anywhere. Playing low is correct if East has a singleton queen. If West has led from 109xxx. East will have a choice of playing the queen or small, either of which gives declarer a ninth trick.

If East plays the nine or ten, declarer can always take the finesse later.

DEAL 125. DECLARE OR DEFEND?

                    ♠ Q 10 6 5
                    ♥ void
                    ♦ K 7 5
                    ♣ K J 10 9 8 4

    ♠ J 4   ♠ K 9 8 7
    ♥ Q 9 5 3   ♥ J 8 7 2
    ♦ 10 9 3 2   ♦ A 6 4
    ♣ 6 5 3   ♣ A 2

                    ♠ A 3 2
                    ♥ A K 10 6 4
                    ♦ Q J 8
                    ♣ Q 7

South	North
1NT	2♠*
2NT	3♥^
3NT	All Pass

*clubs any strength ^shortness

Opening Lead: ♠ Jack

Declarer played the queen from dummy. East, seeing he could set up the spades
covered, planning on returning the spade nine later. But South took the spade ace and
set up the clubs, the spade ten being a later entry. West said "We should have set 3NT
after I made the killing lead."

Do you want to declare or defend? Was West correct?

Yes and no. When South played the queen, East could set 3NT by letting the queen
win. Now South does not have an entry to the clubs. But wait a minute. South can make
3NT by NOT playing the spade queen at Trick 1. Leave the queen and ten in dummy,
win the ace of spades and set up the clubs. Now South has an entry to the clubs.

Which did you choose? Declare or defend?

DEAL 126. A FORK FOR YOUR DUCK

```
                    ♠ K 9 5 4
                    ♥ K 9 3
                    ♦ Q J 6
                    ♣ A 8 7

        ♠ Q J 10 7                    ♠ 8
        ♥ A J 4 2                     ♥ 10 8 7 5
        ♦ 4                           ♦ 3 2
        ♣ K Q J 9                     ♣ 10 6 5 4 3 2

                    ♠ A 6 3 2
                    ♥ Q 6
                    ♦ A K 10 9 8 7 5
                    ♣ void
```

South	West	North	East
1♦	Dbl	Rdbl	2♣
3♦	P	4♣	P
4♠	P	6♦	All Pass

Opening Lead: ♣ King

Declarer played the club ace, discarding a spade. After drawing trumps, led a heart, ducked to the king. He still had to lose a heart and a spade.

Did N/S bid too much or was there a way to make six diamonds?

Declarer went down at Trick 1. He isn't ready to make a discard so should ruff the club and lead a heart. It's a "Morton's Fork"; If West wins South has twelve tricks. If West ducks, West loses his heart as South discards the heart queen on the club ace.

Spades are likely 4-1. Declarer ruffs out the remaining clubs and diamonds and leads a low spade. If West plays low, insert the nine. If East wins and has another spade, spades are 3-2, no problem. If not, East presents you with a ruff/sluff.

If West plays an honor, play low. If East follows, claim. If East shows out, win in hand and lead low to the K9 picking up the suit. If West leads low, play the nine to assure three tricks against any 4-1 split.

131

DEAL 127. STRIP AND ENDPLAY

♠ A 9 7 6
♥ 6 2
♦ J 3
♣ K Q 10 9 6

♠ K Q J 10   ♠ 5 4 2
♥ 4   ♥ J 7 3
♦ A Q 7 4   ♦ 10 9 8 6 2
♣ A 8 7 4   ♣ J 2

♠ 8 3
♥ A K Q 10 9 85
♦ K 5
♣ 5 3

South	West	North	East
1♥	Dbl	Rdbl	P
4♥		All Pass	

Opening Lead: ♠ K

Declarer won the opening lead, drew trumps and led a club to the king. He ruffed a spade and led another club. West won and led another spade. South ruffed but lost two diamonds in the end. Down one.

Was there a better line of play?

Ask yourself- what would you like to happen? You would like West to break the diamond suit or put you in dummy to the good clubs. You can arrange that by removing his safe exit cards which are spades.

So duck the first spade, win the next spade, ruff a spade, draw trumps and lead a club. West must duck so win in dummy and ruff the last spade. When South leads the second club and West wins, he must play a diamond or club.

132

DEAL 128. RECOGNIZING A SECOND SUIT

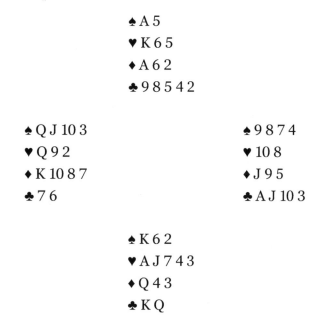

♠ A 5
♥ K 6 5
♦ A 6 2
♣ 9 8 5 4 2

♠ Q J 10 3   ♠ 9 8 7 4
♥ Q 9 2   ♥ 10 8
♦ K 10 8 7   ♦ J 9 5
♣ 7 6   ♣ A J 10 3

♠ K 6 2
♥ A J 7 4 3
♦ Q 4 3
♣ K Q

South opened 1♥ and reached 4♥ after North made a limit raise. West led the ♠Q.

South won the opening lead in dummy, cashed the spade king and ruffed a spade. He cashed the heart king and lost a heart finesse to West's queen. Declarer ruffed the spade return, drew the last trump, led a diamond to the ace and a diamond to his queen, losing to West's king. East got the diamond jack and the club ace, down one.

Unlucky, two losing finesses or was there a better line of play?

Again, hand type. Was this a "finesse" hand or something else? How about a 2nd suit and no finesses? Win the king of spades at Trick 1 and lead the club king. If East wins and returns a spade, declarer wins, takes the club queen, and cashes the A-K of trump ending in dummy.

Now he ruffs a club, ruffs a spade and ruffs another club. The diamond ace is an entry to the good club for a diamond discard, losing one heart, one club, and one diamond.

DEAL 129. A SECOND SUIT IS WHERE YOU FIND ONE

♠ K J 3
♥ A 5 3
♦ J 4
♣ K Q 6 3 2

♠ A 5 2
♥ Q 10 8 7 6
♦ A 7 6
♣ 10 5

♠ 8 7
♥ J 9
♦ 10 9 8 3 2
♣ A J 9 4

♠ Q 10 9 6 4
♥ K 4 2
♦ K Q 5
♣ 8 7

North opened 1♣ and South bid 1♠. North rebid 2♣ and South bid 4♠, West led the ♥7.

South won the first heart with the king and led a trump. West won and led the queen of hearts to dummy's ace. South drew trumps and led the jack of diamonds, but West won, cashed a heart and led a club to East's ace. Down one.

Could declarer have done better?

South has a loser in each suit and must postpone drawing trumps until he can throw a heart loser on a high diamond. Also, South must preserve an entry to his diamond winner by winning

Trick 1 in dummy and leading the jack of diamonds.

If West wins the second diamond and leads a heart, South can win in hand and pitch dummy's last heart on the high diamond. After he ruffs his last heart high, he can start the trumps.

DEAL 130. HANDLING A VOID

♠ 9 8 7 3
♥ K 9
♦ Q 9 3
♣ A J 6 5

♠ 6 5 4   ♠ J 10 2
♥ 8   ♥ 10 6 5 3
♦ J 6 5 4   ♦ K 10
♣ 10 9 8 4 3   ♣ K Q 7 2

♠ A K Q
♥ A Q J 7 4 2
♦ A 8 7 2
♣ void

South opened 2♣, then showed a one suited hand with six or more hearts. North thought he had enough information to bid 6♥. West led the ♣10.

The usual problem- ace opposite a void at Trick 1. What to do? The usual tendency is to win the ace and throw away "something". But what?

Facing three possible diamond losers, declarer won the club ace, throwing a diamond and played for the diamond king to be in West's hand. Even if spades were 3-3, there was no entry.

Down one.

Any suggestions ?

The club ace could be an entry if declarer can force a defender to play one. You can make this hand if the spades are 3-3, and 1) the diamond king is with West, or 2) the diamond king is with East singleton or doubleton. So ruff the opening lead, draw trumps, cash the AKQ of spades, cash the diamond ace and lead a small diamond. If West plays the king, problem solved.

If West plays low, play the queen. If East wins and doesn't have another diamond, he is endplayed to putting you back in the dummy to discard your loser.

If you had won the club ace at Trick 1, you would be going down. That ace is just too valuable as a dummy entry later if the diamonds don't work to relinquish early.

DEAL 131. ANOTHER VOID PROBLEM

```
                    ♠ A J 7 4
                    ♥ 8 7 3
                    ♦ K J 4
                    ♣ 4 3 2

    ♠ K Q 9 8 6 3                    ♠ 10 5 2
    ♥ A Q 2                          ♥ J 6 5 4
    ♦ 9                              ♦ Q
    ♣ K 8 7                          ♣ J 10 9 6 5

                    ♠ void
                    ♥ K 10 9
                    ♦ A 10 8 7 6 5 3 2
                    ♣ A Q
```

South	West	North	East
1♦	1♠	1NT	P
5♦		All Pass	

Opening Lead: ♠ King

Should North-South have been in 3NT? Too late to worry about it now. Let's look at what we have, a common problem. What to do at Trick 1, discard or ruff? But often you don't know what to discard. Declarer won the ace, discarding the club queen, planning to pin his hopes on the heart suit. As you can see, down one when the heart honors were poorly placed for declarer.

Could you have done better?

As a general rule, unless it's an urgent discard, postponing the decision is usually best. You can take the ace later. Ruff the spade, cash the diamond ace and go to dummy with a diamond. Now the spade ace? No!

Lead a heart. If East plays the ace, queen, or jack, you are home. If East plays low, you play the nine. Say West wins with the jack. He is endplayed in three suits.

A spade gives you a free finesse for two discards, a heart gives you the heart king, and a diamond gives you a free finesse. After whichever, I know you can handle the rest. This is a common theme, saving your discard for later when you have more information.

DEAL 132. AVOIDING A DANGER HAND WITH A VOID

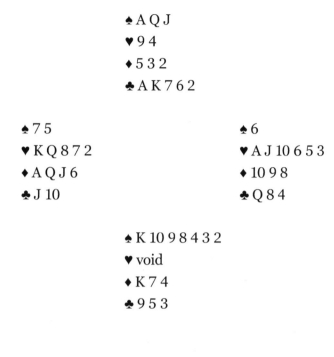

♠ A Q J
♥ 9 4
♦ 5 3 2
♣ A K 7 6 2

♠ 7 5
♥ K Q 8 7 2
♦ A Q J 6
♣ J 10

♠ 6
♥ A J 10 6 5 3
♦ 10 9 8
♣ Q 8 4

♠ K 10 9 8 4 3 2
♥ void
♦ K 7 4
♣ 9 5 3

South	West	North	East
3♠	P	4♠	All
			Pass

Opening Lead: ♥ King

Declarer ruffed the opening lead, drew trumps, and attempted to set up the clubs. She hoped to keep West on lead while doing so but East was able to get in. The lead of the diamond ten meant down one.

Unlucky or was there a better line of play?

This was a danger hand. South was safe as long as West was on lead. Declarer should discard a club at Trick 1. Then when gaining the lead can set up the clubs without letting East in.

***Special Note: If East overtakes the heart king with the ace at trick one, South's plan would fail. Would you find that play?

DEAL 133. L O L

                              ♠ Q 7 4
                              ♥ A K 7
                              ♦ A K 8 6 2
                              ♣ 9 5

        ♠ A J 10 8 6 3   ♠ K 9 5 2
        ♥ 4   ♥ 8
        ♦ 10 3   ♦ Q J 9
        ♣ A Q J 4   ♣ 10 8 7 6 2

                              ♠ void
                              ♥ Q J 10 9 6 5 3 2
                              ♦ 7 5 4
                              ♣ K 3

West opened 1♠ and North overcalled 2♦. East jumped to 3♠ and South bid 4♥. When West bid 4♠, North bid 5♥ which ended the auction. West led the ♠A.

Declarer ruffed and drew trumps.

He then set about establishing the diamonds. However, East won the third diamond and shifted to a club.

Down one.

"Partner," asked North, "Didn't you read Jim and Danny's book 'LOL'?"

What was North referring to? How would you declare?

Declarer should not ruff at Trick 1. Instead discard a diamond on West's ♠A. Now you can set up the diamonds without letting East, the danger hand obtain the lead. And West is in danger of losing his ♣A if he doesn't cash it at Trick 2 to stop an overtrick.

DEFENSE AT TRICK ONE

We have all learned "third hand high" But is this always true? Sometimes, as we will see, it's "third hand not too high". There are lots of deceptive plays, but not too many at Trick 1.

Of course, a sneaky opening lead can often lead declarer astray. There are a few times where underleading an ace against a suit contract is right. But you better be right.

Let's look at some defensive third hand problems at Trick 1.

DEAL 134. HOW HIGH IN THIRD SEAT?

♠ J 8 5
♥ 6 4
♦ Q J 9 7
♣ Q 10 3 2

♠ A 10 2
♥ K Q 10 8 5 2
♦ 4
♣ 9 8 7

South	West	North	East
1♦	P	2♦	2♥
2NT		All Pass	

Opening Lead: ♥ 9

Declarer plays low from dummy. What should East play? South's bid shows about 18-19 HCP's, a strong not a competitive bid. One East played the queen. South ducked and won the continuation with the jack. South started diamonds.

West won the ace but had nothing good to do. West returned a spade, but East's hearts are still not good. Declarer scored two spades, two hearts, two diamonds and in time three clubs.

Could the defense have done better?

Suppose East plays the ten at Trick 1, letting South have his jack. When West leads a diamond, West wins, plays a heart and East can set up the hearts. When in with the spade ace, now East can defeat the contract.

South hand: ♠ K Q   ♥ A J 7   ♦ K 10 8 6 5   ♣ A J 4

DEAL 135. THIRD HAND'S DIFFICULT DECISION

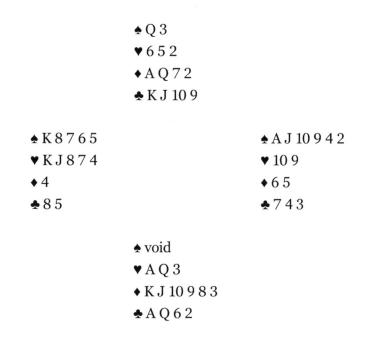

```
                    ♠ Q 3
                    ♥ 6 5 2
                    ♦ A Q 7 2
                    ♣ K J 10 9

   ♠ K 8 7 6 5                       ♠ A J 10 9 4 2
   ♥ K J 8 7 4                       ♥ 10 9
   ♦ 4                               ♦ 6 5
   ♣ 8 5                             ♣ 7 4 3

                    ♠ void
                    ♥ A Q 3
                    ♦ K J 10 9 8 3
                    ♣ A Q 6 2
```

East	South	West	North
2♠	3♦	5♠	6♦

All Pass

Opening Lead: ♠ 6

Declarer played low from dummy, East the ace, and declarer ruffed. While it appears there are two heart tricks to be lost, declarer drew trumps, ran all the clubs ending in dummy and played the spade queen discarding a heart.

West was endplayed. Making six diamonds.

How could the defense have prevailed?

As so often happens, the result was decided at Trick 1. East must play the nine (or ten or jack). South can ruff but since East still has his ace the endplay fails.

141

DEAL 136. THIRD HAND NOT TOO HIGH

♠ A 9 2
♥ K 10 5
♦ A Q 10 6
♣ J 10 8

♠ 7 5   ♠ K 10 8 6 3
♥ J 9 7 4   ♥ Q 6 2
♦ 9 7 3 2   ♦ 8 4
♣ K 6 2   ♣ A 7 5

♠ Q J 4
♥ A 8 3
♦ K J 5
♣ Q 9 4 3

North	East	South	West
1♦	1♠	3NT	All
			Pass

Opening Lead: ♠ 7

Declarer played low from dummy, East took his king and returned the three. South won and led a club. The defense was stuck. If East wins and returns a spade setting up his suit, West has no spade to play when he gets in with his club king.

If West wins the first club, he doesn't have a spade to play. South makes an overtrick. Could the defense do better?

Third hand "high" is a guideline, not a rule. To keep communication, East must leave West with a second spade to lead thru dummy, so he must not win the ♠K and lead another immediately. South can win but now West can win the first club to continue spades.

When East gets in with his club honor, he cashes his good spades. South takes only eight tricks.

DEAL 137. HOW ABOUT THIRD HAND LOW?

                    ♠ A 10 3
                    ♥ J 3
                    ♦ K J 10 7 6 3
                    ♣ 10 8

    ♠ K 4 2   ♠ 9 8 6 5
    ♥ 4   ♥ Q 10 9 8 7
    ♦ A 5 4   ♦ 8 2
    ♣ J 9 7 6 4 2   ♣ A Q

                    ♠ Q J 7
                    ♥ A K 6 5 2
                    ♦ Q 9
                    ♣ K 5 3

North opened a Weak 2♦ bid and South bid 2NT, trying for game and asking for a feature, any outside ace or king. When North bid 3♠, South bid 3NT. West led the ♣6.

East won the ace at Trick 1 and returned the queen. Declarer played low so East switched to a low heart. Declarer won and after forcing out the diamond ace took a spade finesse for ten tricks.

Could the defense have possibly defeated the contract?

We are by now familiar with playing the queen in third seat from AQx, but how about playing low, the queen from AQ doubleton? The same problem exists for South, win or duck?

South made the normal play of winning the king, to avoid going down three if West had led from AJ7642 and started the diamonds. West held up till the third round. This allowed East to unblock the club ace, and West ran the clubs.

DEAL 138. HIGH OR NOT TOO HIGH

                          ♠ J 8 3
                          ♥ K 9 3
                          ♦ J 8 2
                          ♣ A Q 5 4

        ♠ 10 7 4   ♠ 9 6 5
        ♥ J 8 2   ♥ 10 7 6 5
        ♦ ? ? 7 4   ♦ K 9 3
        ♣ 10 7 2   ♣ K 9 6

                          ♠ K Q 2 ?
                          ♥ A Q 4
                          ♦ ? 6 5
                          ♣ J 8 3

South	West	North	East
1NT	P	3NT	All Pass

Opening Lead: ♦ 4

Declarer plays low from dummy. Should East play the king or the nine? Well, it depends. If West has led from Q1074, East should play the nine. If West has led from AQ74, East should play the king. So what's it going to be? The fate of 3NT is at stake. One declarer played the nine, declarer had 1065 and won the ten and had nine tricks.

Should East have played the king?

Another defender played the king, declarer won the ace from A65. What's going on?

No, bridge is not a perfect game. Some things can be worked out at the table, some not. Even the best players can go wrong when the facts are not clear. This hand is just made up to show sometimes there is no right answer. Declarer could have had either ♦A65 or ♦1065.

My friend Danny has an answer for this. He thinks leads from four card suits headed by aces are undesirable, a last resort. Trusting West would have sooner made a passive lead from, say ten-third than ♦AQxx, East should credit West with ♦Q10xx and insert the ♦9.

DEAL 139. NOT TOO HIGH TO HELP PARTNER

```
                    ♠ 10 8 3
                    ♥ A 9 7 6 4
                    ♦ K 9
                    ♣ 6 5 2

  ♠ K J 9 7 5                      ♠ A Q 2
  ♥ 8 2                            ♥ Q 5
  ♦ J 4 3                          ♦ 8 7 6 5
  ♣ A Q 4                          ♣ 10 9 8 3

                    ♠ 5 4
                    ♥ K J 10 3
                    ♦ A Q 10 2
                    ♣ K J 7
```

South	West	North	East
1♦	1♠	Dbl	2♠
3♥		All Pass	

Opening Lead: ♠ 7

East won the spade ace and returned the ten of clubs. West won the trick but was unsure he could return a low spade. After cashing the spade king, the defense was finished. The defense got two spades and only two clubs. The declarer was able to discard one of dummy's clubs on his diamonds.

How could the defense have done better?

If the lead is 4th best, using the Rule of Eleven, South does not have a higher spade. East can help West by playing the spade queen at trick one.

Then when West wins his first club trick, he knows he can lead a low spade to East for another club thru, scoring two spades and three clubs. Partners need help.

DEAL 140. THIRD HAND NOT TOO HIGH

```
              ♠ Q 10 2
              ♥ K 6
              ♦ 10 9 7 6 2
              ♣ K J 4

  ♠ J 8 6 3              ♠ K 7 5 4
  ♥ 10 8 7 3             ♥ 9 4 2
  ♦ 8                    ♦ A K 4
  ♣ A 9 8 6              ♣ 5 3 2

              ♠ A 9
              ♥ A Q J 5
              ♦ Q J 5 3
              ♣ Q 10 7
```

South opened 1NT, North bid 3NT, and West led the ♠3.

Declarer played low from dummy, East played the king (third hand high), and declarer won the ace. Declarer started the diamonds but with two more spade stoppers, was able to take ten tricks.

How could the defense have prevailed?

Sitting East, at Trick 1, you should consider there is a good chance South has the spade ace, and to keep your king "over" dummy's queen, just play your seven.

"Good chance?" Applying Danny's Guideline, it's a near certainty. But if West has led from ♠Axxx or ♠AJxx, when you get in with a diamond and return the ♠4, the defense will get the three spade tricks it has coming. Before cashing the last one you will cash a second diamond to beat 3NT. The ♠7 is a "can gain, can't cost" play.

Declarer will win the nine but now has only two spade tricks instead of three.

When East wins the first diamond, she will return the spade four to declarer's ace. Upon winning the second diamond, on this layout the defense has five tricks: two spades, two diamonds, and one club.

DEAL 141. MORE OF THE SAME

```
              ♠ 5 2
              ♥ K J 7
              ♦ A 9 5 3 2
              ♣ K 10 4

♠ J 10 8 7 6                    ♠ A Q 9
♥ 6 5 4                         ♥ Q 3 2
♦ Q J                           ♦ 10 7
♣ 9 8 7                         ♣ J 6 5 3 2

              ♠ K 4 3
              ♥ A 10 9 8
              ♦ K 8 6 4
              ♣ A Q
```

After another 1NT - 3NT auction, West led the ♠J.

East won the ace at Trick 1 and returned the queen. Declarer ducked and won the third round of spades. Before testing diamonds, declarer lost a heart finesse to East, the "safe" hand, and had the rest.

Was there a better defense?

Perhaps. Look what happens after East correctly plays the ♠Q at Trick 1. Declarer can't afford to duck so he wins and tests diamonds. When they split 2-2, he unblocks his clubs, cashes three more diamonds and the ♣K, discarding his two low spades.

In the four-card ending declarer cashes dummy's ♥K for his tenth trick and can now finesse East for the ♥Q, taking thirteen tricks. East's good play cost himself three IMP's but if diamonds did not split and declarer needed the heart finesse, it was the correct play to defeat 3NT.

Hey, that's bridge.

DEAL 142. NOT TOO HIGH AGAINST A SUIT CONTRACT

```
                          ♠ A 10 8
                          ♥ J 6 5
                          ♦ K 8 5
                          ♣ K J 7 4

        ♠ 5 3                            ♠ K 6
        ♥ Q 9 7 2                        ♥ A 10 8 4
        ♦ J 6 3 2                        ♦ A Q 10 9
        ♣ 10 8 3                         ♣ 9 6 2

                          ♠ Q J 9 7 4 2
                          ♥ K 3
                          ♦ 7 4
                          ♣ A Q 5
```

North opened 1♣ and rebid 1NT after South bid 1♠. South bid 4♠. West led the ♥2.

Dummy played low, East won the ace and returned a heart. Declarer won and lost a trump finesse. He ruffed the heart return, drew trumps and ran the clubs to pitch a diamond, losing one diamond in the end.

Was there a better defense?

East has thirteen HCP's so there is little left for West. Unfortunately, West didn't lead a diamond. But maybe a second chance? Desperate measures are called for. If East plays the heart ten at Trick 1, maybe he can get West in after he wins the trump king? Worth a try, no?

Of course if South should happen to play dummy's jack at Trick 1, skip this deal and go to the next page please.

DEAL 143. HOW HIGH AND WHY?

♠ J 9 4
♥ A 7 5
♦ Q 6
♣ K Q 10 8 7

♠ K 8 7 2
♥ 6 4 2
♦ K 10 8
♣ 6 5 3

South	North
1NT	3NT

Opening Lead: ♦5

Declarer plays low. What should East play? One East, to keep the king over the queen, played the nine. Declarer won the jack and took eleven tricks.

Could the defense have done better?

The Rule of Eleven tells East declarer has only one honor card higher than the five, so it's either the ace or the jack. If it's the ace, what would declarer have played from dummy at Trick 1?

What would you have played if you were South?

South's hand: ♠ A Q 10 9   ♥ K Q 10 9   ♦ J 2   ♣ A J 2

DEAL 144. HOW HIGH? WHY?

♠ J 4 3
♥ A Q J 8
♦ 7 6
♣ J 7 6 4

♠ K 9 6
♥ 9 5 2
♦ A 9 8
♣ K Q 9 8

East	South	West	North
1♣	1NT	P	2♣
P	2♦	P	2NT
P	3NT	All Pass	

Opening Lead: ♠ 5

Declarer plays low from dummy. What should East play? The Rule of Eleven says South has two higher spades than the five. The king is right if West has the A-Q; the nine if West has the Q-10.

East tossed a coin and put up the king.

Was this a coin toss or should East figure out the answer?

If you do the simple math, how many points can West have? South said he had a maximum, seventeen or eighteen. The most West can have is one or two, either the ♠Q, the ♦Q, or the ♦J.

I'd bet it's the ♠Q, wouldn't you?.

West's spades: ♠ Q 10 7 5 2   South's spades: ♠ A 8

The spade lead is the killer but only if East plays the nine.

150

DEAL 145. THIRD HAND GIVES FALSE COUNT

♠ Q J 7
♥ Q 9 8 6
♦ A Q
♣ 9 8 5 2

♠ A K 9 4   ♠ 10 5 3 2
♥ 2   ♥ A 10 7 3
♦ 10 9 8 2   ♦ 6 4 3
♣ Q 10 4 3   ♣ 7 6

♠ 8 6
♥ K J 5 4
♦ K J 7 5
♣ A K J

South	West	North	East
1NT	P	2♣	P
2♥	P	4♥	All Pass

Opening Lead: ♠ Ace

East play the spade five at Trick 1, leaving West unsure of how to continue. West switched to the diamond ten. Despite the 4-1 trump split, declarer had ten tricks.

Was there a way to promote another trick for the defense?

East should be trying to get a trump promotion. If he plays the spade ten at Trick 1, looking like he wants to ruff the third round, West will continue spades playing king and another. But East follows. When East wins the second round of hearts, here are the trumps that remain:

North ♥ 9 8

     East ♥ 10 7

South ♥ J 5

Now East plays his last spade. Wherever declarer ruffs, East scores another trump.

DEAL 146. ENCOURAGE OR OVERTAKE ?

```
              ♠ 8 5 4
              ♥ Q 7 3
              ♦ K J 3
              ♣ 5 4 3 2

  ♠ Q J                      ♠ 9
  ♥ J 10 9 2                 ♥ A K 8 5 4
  ♦ Q 8 7                    ♦ 10 6 5 4 2
  ♣ A Q J 9                  ♣ 10 7

              ♠ A K 10 7 6 3 2
              ♥ 6
              ♦ A 9
              ♣ K 8 6
```

West	North	East	South
1♣	P	1♥	1♠
2♥*	2♠	P	4♠

*4-card support playing support doubles with 3

Opening Lead:　　♥ Jack

South ducked the opening lead, East played an encouraging eight. Declarer ruffed the second round, drew trumps, and took a diamond finesse to discard one club loser. Making four spades. Painful.

How should the defense have played?

East knows South has only one heart from the bidding. It's a simple matter of overtaking at Trick 1 to shift to a club. Mike Lawrence pointed out in the ACBL Bulletin, April 2020, other possible club positions where overtaking with the ♥A would be necessary include:

West: ♣ AJ98　　South: ♣ KQ6

Also a more difficult overtake position is when the heart king is in dummy, East has just the ace, and the clubs are: West: ♣ AQ97　　South: 　♣ K86　　East: ♣ J10

East has to win the ace at Trick 1 and shift to a club at Trick 2.

DEAL 147. THIRD HAND UNBLOCKS

♠ K 7 6 3
♥ Q J 4 2
♦ A
♣ Q 8 6 2

♠ 10 8   ♠ Q J 9 2
♥ 9 7 3   ♥ 10 8 6 5
♦ K 9 7 6 2   ♦ Q J 8
♣ K 7 3   ♣ 5 4

♠ A 5 4
♥ A K
♦ 10 5 4 3
♣ A J 10 9

South opened 1NT. North bid 2♣, Stayman, looking for a major fit, then signed off in 3NT.

West led the ♦6.

Dummy's ace won the first trick perforce. Declarer took a club finesse, losing to West's king. West continued with a low diamond. East won the trick.
Now what?
If you were East, did you unblock your diamond queen under the ace?
If you unblocked the jack at Trick 1, West will properly interpret it as denying the queen and won't continue diamonds at all. If you play the eight, you blocked the suit. The queen is the correct play at Trick 1.
If you have the diamond eight left in your hand, E/W can run the diamonds. If you are sitting there having won the trick with an honor and don't have the eight, don't tell anyone.

DEAL 148. LISTEN TO THE BIDDING AND DUCK

```
                    ♠ Q 10 7 4
                    ♥ 6 3
                    ♦ K J 9 4
                    ♣ A 9 5

        ♠ K 9 6                        ♠ 3 2
        ♥ Q 9 7                        ♥ K 10 5 2
        ♦ 10 2                         ♦ A 8 5 3
        ♣ 10 7 6 4 3                   ♣ J 8 2

                    ♠ A J 8 5
                    ♥ A J 8 4
                    ♦ Q 7 6
                    ♣ K Q
```

South	West	North	East
1NT	P	2♣	P
2♥	P	3NT	P
4♠		All Pass	

Opening Lead: ♦ 10

East won the first trick with the ace and returned the diamond eight, hoping to give West a ruff, and suit preference for hearts. Declarer won, lost a trump finesse, won the heart return and made four spades, losing one diamond, one heart, and one spade.

Could the defense have done better?

The bidding marked South with at least eight cards in the majors. If the opening lead was a singleton, that would give declarer a shape like 4414, unlikely. If East ducks the first trick, hoping West has a fast entry, he can win the second diamond and give West a diamond ruff for down one.

154

DEAL 149. AVOIDING DECLARER'S
LOSER-ON-LOSER PLAY

```
                    ♠ Q 9 4
                    ♥ J 10 9 2
                    ♦ Q 10
                    ♣ K 9 8 7

    ♠ 8                          ♠ 7
    ♥ K 8 5                      ♥ A Q 7 6 4 3
    ♦ K J 9 8 6 3                ♦ 7 5 2
    ♣ 10 6 3                     ♣ A Q J

                    ♠ A K J 10 6 5 3 2
                    ♥ void
                    ♦ A 4
                    ♣ 5 4 2
```

East	South	West	North
1♥	1♠	2♥	2♠
4♥	4♠	All Pass	

Opening Lead: ♥ 5

South should have bid 4♠ directly over East's opening bid, making it harder for East-West to find a cheap 5♥ save. But South should have been punished even more.

Declarer played low from dummy, East the ace and declarer ruffed. Keeping low trumps in hand, declarer went to dummy and led a heart discarding a club. West won and switched to a club, losing to East's jack. East returned a diamond.

Declarer won the ace, went again to dummy with a low trump and with a ruffing finesse was able to set up a heart to discard a loser. Making four spades.

How could the defense have prevailed after the heart lead?

Declarer is marked with a void in hearts on the bidding so there is no point for East to play the ace at Trick 1. Any low heart will suffice and now South lacks the entries and communication to set up a heart to get rid of a loser. With a direct 4♠ bid, East would not know South is void.

DEAL 150. ENCOURAGE OR TAKE OVER

                    ♠ 10 5 4
                    ♥ 9 2
                    ♦ A K Q
                    ♣ K J 7 5 3

    ♠ 7 6   ♠ 9 8 2
    ♥ K Q 5 4   ♥ A 10 8 3
    ♦ 9 7 4   ♦ 10 8 6 3 2
    ♣ 10 9 6 2   ♣ A

                    ♠ A K Q J 3
                    ♥ J 7 6
                    ♦ J 5
                    ♣ Q 8 4

South opened 1♠ and North bid 2♣, game forcing. South bid 3♣ and North bid 3♠.
South ended the auction at 4♠. West led the ♥King.

East signaled encouragement with the ten. Whether West continues the heart
queen or a low heart, the defense was finished. Declarer lost two hearts and one club,
making four spades.

Whose fault was this?

Who is the boss here? East should look at the whole deal. Overtake the heart king
with his ace. Now cash the club ace and play a heart to partner's queen.

If partner doesn't give you a club ruff now for down one, call me and I'll help you
find a new partner.

DEAL 151. ENCOURAGE OR DO WHAT?

♠ J 10 8 3
♥ 6 3
♦ A K
♣ Q J 10 9 7

♠ 6 5
♥ A J 7 5 4
♦ Q 10 9 5 3
♣ 3

West	North	East	South
1♥	Dbl	4♥	4♠
	All Pass		

Opening Lead: ♥ King

East encouraged with the jack. West played another heart, South ruffed. South lost a trick to the ace of trumps and the club king, making four spades.

How should East have played?

Forget encouraging. Do things yourself. You need a club ruff and if West has an entry (he did open the bidding), overtake at Trick 1 and play your singleton. If West has the club ace, or the club king and the spade ace, you will defeat the contract with a club ruff.

West's hand: ♠ A 7   ♥ K Q 10 8 2   ♦ J 2   ♣ K 8 5 4

South's hand: ♠ K Q 9 4 2   ♥ 9   ♦ 8 7 6 4   ♣ A 6 2

DEAL 152. ENCOURAGE OR ?

        ♠ 9 7 2
        ♥ Q 8 5
        ♦ 7 3
        ♣ A Q 10 8 2

♠ A Q 5   ♠ 6 3
♥ J 7 2   ♥ K 9 4
♦ Q J 9 4   ♦ K 10 8 5
♣ 9 4 3   ♣ K J 7 5

        ♠ K J 10 8 4
        ♥ A 10 6 3
        ♦ A 6 2
        ♣ 6

South opened 1♠ and North raised to 2♠. Had he been a passed hand, East might have balanced with a take-out double. West led the ♦Queen.

Declarer played low from dummy, East encouraged with the ten and declarer ducked. He won the diamond continuation and ruffed a diamond in dummy.

Declarer then started the trumps. He lost two trumps and two hearts.

Making two spades.

With better defense, South should have gone down one. How?

East knew he had the club suit under control but thought declarer might need a diamond ruff. At Trick 1, he overtook the diamond queen with his king to play a trump.

What could declarer do? If he ducked, West would win and play three rounds of trumps. If he won Trick 1,

East had the diamond ten to obtain the lead and play a trump. Either way, no diamond ruff for the declarer.

Down one.

DEAL 153. NO HURRY, JUST ENCOURAGE

                           ♠ K 5 4
                           ♥ A 4
                           ♦ K J 6
                           ♣ J 10 9 8 2

        ♠ Q J 8 7 2   ♠ 10 9
        ♥ 5 2   ♥ K J 10 7 6 3
        ♦ 8 7 5 4   ♦ 9 3 2
        ♣ K 5   ♣ A 6

                           ♠ A 6 3
                           ♥ Q 9 8
                           ♦ A Q 10
                           ♣ Q 7 4 3

North opened 1♣ and East made a Weak Jump Overcall of 2♥, although some might
bid 1♥. South bid what he thought he could make, 3NT. West led the ♥ 5.

Declarer played low from dummy and East won his king. He returned another
heart. Declarer started the clubs. It didn't matter who won the first club. East was
never going to run his hearts. Declarer won ten tricks:
   two spades, two hearts, three diamonds, and three clubs.
   "Partner," said West, "I have a book for you to read called 'Second Hand High,
Third Hand Not So High'."
   What was West referring to? How should East have defended?
   There is a song that starts "Fools rush in." East was in too much of a hurry at Trick
1. To preserve the linkage between the defenders and the timing, South should merely
encourage with the ♥7, knowing declarer surely has ♥Qxx from the bidding.
   South takes the queen and starts the clubs, but West will win the first club and
continue hearts.
   East still has the club ace and can cash the hearts. Down two.

DEAL 154. ENCOURAGE THE BEST YOU CAN

                         ♠ K Q J 10
                         ♥ K 6 4
                         ♦ A 7 6 3
                         ♣ 6 3

        ♠ A 9 2   ♠ 8 5.
        ♥ 9 8   ♥ A Q 5 3 2
        ♦ Q 9 4 2   ♦ 10 5
        ♣ J 9 7 4   ♣ 10 8 2

                         ♠ 7 6 4
                         ♥ J 10 7
                         ♦ K J 8
                         ♣ A K Q 5

South	West	North	East
1♣	P	1♦	P
1NT	P	3NT	All Pass

Opening Lead: ♥ 9

At Trick 1 with only low cards to go with the A-Q, East won the queen, then the ace, then played another heart. After that start declarer had no trouble making 3NT, West never being able to reach East.

How would you have defended?

A five isn't a very encouraging looking card but that's what they dealt you so the five it is. Let declarer win the first trick. This caters to West having started with more than one heart and being able to get in to continue the suit.

You wish you had a more encouraging card but, hey, that's what you got, that's what you play.

DEAL 155. WIN OR DUCK?

                        ♠ K 7 4
                        ♥ Q 10 2
                        ♦ 8 7
                        ♣ K Q 10 7 3

    ♠ 10 6   ♠ A Q 8 5 3
    ♥ 8 6 5 4   ♥ J 9 3
    ♦ 9 5 3 2   ♦ Q 10 6 4
    ♣ A 9 2   ♣ 4

                        ♠ J 9 2
                        ♥ A K 7
                        ♦ A K J
                        ♣ J 8 6 5

South   North

1NT   3NT

Opening Lead: ♠ 10

Hoping to find partner's suit, West made a great lead of the spade ten. Dummy played low but East played the queen. East shifted to a diamond.

After knocking out the two aces, South made 4NT. West was not happy after his inspired lead.

How should East have defended after West's good lead?

East should duck the first trick. Aren't you getting tired of hearing this? Now when West gets in with the club ace and leads his last spade, West takes four spade tricks for down one.

DEAL 156. DIFFICULT DUCK

♠ Q 8 5
♥ A 9
♦ K J 4
♣ Q J 10 9 4

♠ 7 6 3 2　　　　　　　　　♠ A Q 8 5 3
♥ 5 2　　　　　　　　　　♥ J 9 3
♦ 8 6 5 3 2　　　　　　　♦ Q 10 6 4
♣ A 6　　　　　　　　　　♣ 4

♠ A K 10
♥ J 10 4 3
♦ A Q 10
♣ 8 5 3

North	East	South	West
1♣	1♥	3NT	All Pass

Opening Lead:　♥ 5

Dummy played the nine, East won the queen and returned a heart to the ace. Declarer led the club queen, West winning the ace. Declarer won the spade shift, lost a club to the king, lost one more heart and had the rest.

Could the defense have prevailed?

South's bidding suggests J-10-x-x in hearts and if declarer also has the club ace, the contract can't be defeated. To give himself a chance and maintain communication, East must let the heart nine win the first trick.

West will get in and leads his last heart, and when East gets in with the club king, the defense has five tricks.

DEAL 157. HIDING WHAT YOU HAVE

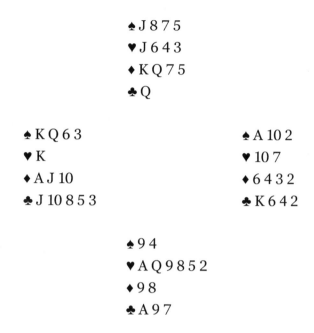

♠J875
♥J643
♦KQ75
♣Q

♠KQ63
♥K
♦AJ10
♣J10853

♠A102
♥107
♦6432
♣K642

♠94
♥AQ9852
♦98
♣A97

West	North	East	South
1♣	P	1NT	2♥
P	4♥	All Pass	

West led the ♣4. East covered dummy's queen with the king and declarer won the ace. Judging that the AK of spades were divided from the opening lead, declarer played West for the trump king and laid down the ♥Ace.

Making four hearts. "Well done, partner," said North.

"Hold your hand back, partner," said East.

How would you have defended to defeat the contract?

As East, play low at Trick 1. Declarer will probably place the club king with West. If East had one spade honor, it was logical she could have the trump king for her bid. Declarer will likely take a 'normal' trump finesse.

Down one.

DEAL 158. DEFENDER'S FALSECARD

                    ♠ 10 8 3
                    ♥ Q 7 5 4
                    ♦ K Q 4 3
                    ♣ K 7

    ♠ J 6 5 2   ♠ A K 4
    ♥ 10 6   ♥ J 9
    ♦ J 8 5 2   ♦ 10 9 7 6
    ♣ A 8 6   ♣ 9 5 3 2

                    ♠ Q 9 7
                    ♥ A K 8 3 2
                    ♦ A
                    ♣ Q J 10 4

South opened 1♥ and North bid 3♥, a limit raise. South bid 4♥.

West led the ♠2.

East won the king, then ace of spades and played a third spade. Declare won, drew trumps, lost a club and made four hearts.

What might have happened to defeat four hearts?

Suppose East won the opening lead with the ace, South playing the nine. East knew South had at least three spades & returned the four as he would from ♠AJ64. If West has the jack or queen, South will probably lose three spade tricks.

On the actual layout, South had to guess and played low on the second spade. If East wins the king at Trick 1, South can't go wrong.

DEAL 159. GIVING FALSE SIGNALS

♠ K 10 8 4
♥ A K J 3
♦ 7 3
♣ Q 9 3

♠ 3
♥ 10 8 6 4
♦ 6 5 2
♣ A K 8 7 6

♠ A J 9
♥ 7 5 2
♦ Q 9 8 4
♣ 10 5 2

♠ Q 7 6 5 2
♥ Q 9
♦ A K J 10
♣ J 4

North	East	South	West
		1♠	P
2NT*	P	4♠^	All Pass

*Forcing spade raise ^minimum, no shortness

Opening Lead: ♣ Ace

East played the club two at Trick 1 and West switched. Declarer was able to discard his other club loser, making four spades.

How could the defense have prevented this?

East, looking at two trump tricks, wanted West to take the A-K of clubs if possible so she played the club ten at Trick 1. West, thinking she was going to give East a club ruff continued with the club king and another. She was confused when East followed to the third club but when declarer went down one, all was forgiven.

"I didn't know we had switched to upside down count," said West, smiling.

165

DEAL 160. WIN OR DUCK?

           ♠ K 8 5
           ♥ A 10 7 6 5
           ♦ 7 6
           ♣ 9 5 4

♠ 9 6   ♠ A 4 2
♥ K Q 2   ♥ 9 8 4 3
♦ K Q 10 9 8   ♦ 3 2
♣ J 8 2   ♣ 10 7 6 3

           ♠ Q J 10 7 3
           ♥ J
           ♦ A J 5 4
           ♣ A K Q

South	West	North	East
1♠	P	2♠	P
3♦	P	4♠	All Pass

Opening Lead: ♠ 6

This is a classic situation for a trump lead. West suspected declarer would be ruffing diamonds in dummy. East won the spade ace and returned a trump.

Declarer won the second trump, played ace and a diamond. She eventually got to ruff one diamond in dummy, making four spades.

Could the defense have prevailed?

West got off to a good start. East must duck the first trump lead. When West gets in with his diamond king, he can return a second trump.

Now East can win and play a third round of trumps. No ruff for you Mrs. Declarer. Down one.

DEAL 161. WHY COUNT IS SO IMPORTANT

♠ 10 7 6
♥ A K 10 9
♦ Q J 10 9
♣ J 2

♠ A Q 9 5 4
♥ 8 5
♦ K 2
♣ 8 6 4 3

♠ 8 3 2
♥ J 7 6 3
♦ 7 4
♣ K 10 9 5

♠ K J
♥ Q 4 2
♦ A 8 6 5 3
♣ A Q J 7

South	West	North	East
1NT	P	2♣	P
2♦	P	3NT	All Pass

Opening Lead: ♠ 5

The first trick went 5, 6, 8, jack. Declarer played a heart to the board and took a losing diamond finesse. West was uncertain how to continue. Picturing a possible South hand like:

♠KJ3   ♥QJ2   ♦A8653   ♦KQ   West played a high club at Trick 4. South now had one spade, three hearts, four diamonds and two clubs.

How could the defense have avoided this disaster?

East cannot possibly gain by playing the eight to cover the six at Trick 1. Much more important is to give West the count, the attitude being known when East can't play a high card. So East has one or three spades.

Now West will know South started with a doubleton spade (it can't be four from the auction). West will lay down the spade ace and take his four spade tricks. Down one.

DEAL 162. THE IMPORTANCE OF COUNT

♠ Q J 8
♥ Q J 10 8
♦ 10 6 2
♣ K J 4

♠ K 7 5 2
♥ A 3
♦ 8 7 5 3
♣ A 5 2

South	North
1NT	2♣
2♦	3NT

***** THE ABOVE HANDS ARE WEST AND NORTH

Opening Lead: ♠ 2

Declarer wins the queen in dummy, East playing the three, and leads the club king to West's ace. How should you, West, continue?

The actual West exited passively with a diamond. Declarer knocked out the heart ace and took nine tricks.

Could the defense have done better? Compare this to the previous hand.

West lacked a crucial piece of information. How many spades did South start with? If two (Ax), West can play a low spade at Trick 3, dropping South's ace. So it's crucial that East, unable to beat the dummy, gives count.

The actual East started with 10943 of spades and should play the ten at Trick 1. That has to be an even number, two or four. West knows from the auction South does not have four spades so if West has four, South now has the bare ace. West will exit a spade at Trick 3. The defense will score two spades and their three aces.

East's hand: ♠ 10 9 4 3   ♥ 7 6 5 2   ♦ A 9 4   ♣ 9 8
South's hand: ♠ A 6   ♥ K 9 4   ♦ K Q J   ♣ Q 10 7 6 3

DEAL 163. ONE MORE ON THE IMPORTANCE OF COUNT

♠ Q J 3
♥ Q 9 2
♦ K J 4 2
♣ J 4 3

♠ K 9 7 6 5
♥ J 7 5
♦ A 7
♣ 9 8 6

♠ 10 4
♥ K 4 3
♦ 9 8 6 3
♣ A 7 5 2

♠ A 8 2
♥ A 10 8 6
♦ Q 10 5
♣ K Q 10

South	North
1NT	3NT

Opening Lead: ♠ 6

Declarer played dummy's queen, East the four. Declarer now led the heart nine to West's jack. West played another low spade, dummy's jack winning. A successful heart finesse followed and after knocking out the diamond ace declarer had nine tricks.

Three spades, three hearts, and three diamonds.

Whose fault was this?

100% East. Remember, this is a count situation because West knows immediately that East has no strength in the suit. When East played the four of spades at Trick 1, West assumed East had three spade so declarer must have started with Ax. If so it was safe to exit a low spade and drop South's ace.

If East had played the ten at Trick 1, West would have known a spade at Trick 3 was wrong.

The nine of clubs would have been a reasonable guess as the right shift. East would win the ace and return his remaining spade. Now West gets in with the diamond ace and runs the spades.

169

DEAL 164. COUNT WHEN DEFENDING AGAINST A SLAM

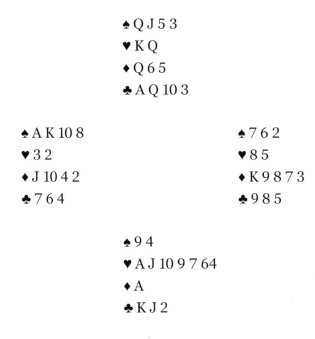

```
                    ♠ Q J 5 3
                    ♥ K Q
                    ♦ Q 6 5
                    ♣ A Q 10 3

    ♠ A K 10 8                      ♠ 7 6 2
    ♥ 3 2                           ♥ 8 5
    ♦ J 10 4 2                      ♦ K 9 8 7 3
    ♣ 7 6 4                         ♣ 9 8 5

                    ♠ 9 4
                    ♥ A J 10 9 7 64
                    ♦ A
                    ♣ K J 2
```

South	West	North	East
1♥	P	1♠	P	*Cue bid for hearts
3♥	P	4♣*	P	
6♥	All Pass			

Opening Lead: ♠ King

West led the spade king, East played the two, declarer the nine. Believing the bidding and seeing the spade two, West switched to a club and the slam rolled home.

What should defender's cards mean against a slam?

Against a slam if opening leader leads a king, partner should give count, telling how many he has. Attitude is almost always obvious or known.

Playing ace from A-K is for partials and games, the king is led against slams.

DEAL 165. SUIT PREFERENCE SIGNALS

```
                        ♠ Q J 5 4
                        ♥ A 7 5 2
                        ♦ A K 3
                        ♣ 7 5

        ♠ A K 7                         ♠ 10 6 3 2
        ♥ K J 9 3                       ♥ Q 8
        ♦ 5 4                           ♦ 10 6 2
        ♣ A Q J 10                      ♣ 8 6 4 2

                        ♠ 9 8
                        ♥ 10 6 4
                        ♦ Q J 9 8 7
                        ♣ K 9 3
```

West	North	East	South
1♣	Dbl	P	1♦
Dbl	P	1♠	2♦
			All Pass

Opening Lead: ♠ Ace

West led the spade ace, East playing the two. West, afraid that South had a singleton spade, shifted to a trump. Declarer won and led the spade nine, West won and played another trump.

South won and had eight tricks.

Could the defense have done better?

At Trick 1, East's card is critical. The attitude is known. The count can't be relevant so West needs to switch. East should play the ten of spades at Trick 1 to get a heart shift before declarer sets up the Q-J of spades for discards.

171

DEAL 166. UNUSUAL SUIT PREFERENCE AT TRICK ONE

```
                        ♠ 9 6 2
                        ♥ Q 10 9
                        ♦ A K Q 9 4
                        ♣ K 2

        ♠ 7 5 3                        ♠ A 4
        ♥ A K 5                        ♥ J 6 4 3 2
        ♦ 10 8 5 2                     ♦ 6
        ♣ 10 9 5                       ♣ J 7 6 4 3

                        ♠ K Q J 10 8
                        ♥ 8 7
                        ♦ J 7 3
                        ♣ A Q 8
```

South	West	North	East
1♠	P	2♦	P
2♠	P	4♠	All PASS

Playing ace from AK, West led the heart ace, East played low and West shifted to a club. Declarer drove out the ace of trumps, lost a second heart and took the rest.

Was there a better play available to the defense?

Suit preference at Trick 1 is not common. But the attitude here is known, the queen being in the dummy. East must play the heart jack at Trick 1.

This can't be shortness; that would give South five or six hearts so it must be suit preference for an unlikely but necessary diamond shift.

When East gets in with the trump ace, he can return a heart to West. A diamond ruff is the setting trick.

DEAL 167. A DIFFICULT SUIT PREFERENCE

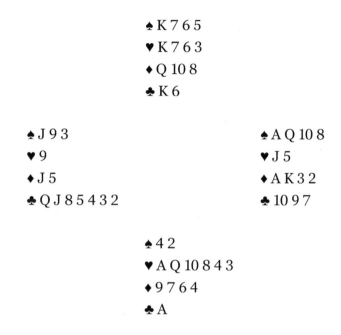

$\spadesuit$ K 7 6 5
$\heartsuit$ K 7 6 3
$\diamondsuit$ Q 10 8
$\clubsuit$ K 6

$\spadesuit$ J 9 3
$\heartsuit$ 9
$\diamondsuit$ J 5
$\clubsuit$ Q J 8 5 4 3 2

$\spadesuit$ A Q 10 8
$\heartsuit$ J 5
$\diamondsuit$ A K 3 2
$\clubsuit$ 10 9 7

$\spadesuit$ 4 2
$\heartsuit$ A Q 10 8 4 3
$\diamondsuit$ 9 7 6 4
$\clubsuit$ A

East	South	West	North	
1$\diamondsuit$	1$\heartsuit$	P	2$\diamondsuit$	* Overbid; cue bid was fine, but enough
P	2$\heartsuit$	P	3$\heartsuit$*	
	All Pass			

Opening Lead: $\diamondsuit$ Jack

East covered the queen with the king, cashed the ace, and gave West a diamond ruff. West stared at that diamond three, a pretty low card for a long time and finally played back a club.

Declarer claimed.

Any ideas?

Maybe. East should anticipate the problem. If he goes out of his way to play the diamond ace first, then king, before giving West a ruff, there is a chance West will return a spade.

173

DEAL 168. ATTITUDE? COUNT? WHAT?

```
                    ♠ 10 7
                    ♥ A 8 6 4 3
                    ♦ J 5 3
                    ♣ A J 2

      ♠ J 3                         ♠ Q 9 6 5
      ♥ 2                           ♥ Q J 7
      ♦ A K 10 8 6 4                ♦ 7 2
      ♣ Q 9 8 3                     ♣ K 10 5 4

                    ♠ A K 8 4 2
                    ♥ K 10 9 5
                    ♦ Q 9
                    ♣ 7 6
```

South	West	North	East
1♠	2♦	Dbl	P
2♥	P	3♥	P
4♥		All Pass	

Opening Lead: ♦ Ace

The first trick went ace, three, seven, nine. West continued with the king, everyone following.

Seeing East's high-low, West continued with a low diamond. East ruffed with the heart jack while South discarded a club.

South won the return, drew trumps, and made four hearts.

Was there a better line of defense?

East has a trump trick coming but wants a club shift, not more diamonds. She should discourage at Trick 1 by playing the two. After this attitude signal, West will make the obvious shift to a club. South loses one club, two diamonds, and one trump.

DEAL 169. LITTLE TRUMPS CAN MEAN A LOT

♠ 8 7
♥ Q 3
♦ 9 7 5
♣ A 7 6 4 3 2

♠ 6 5 2
♥ J 9 7 6 4
♦ K 8 2
♣ Q 8

♠ 9 3
♥ 5 2
♦ J 10 6 4 3
♣ K J 10 9

♠ A K Q J 10 4
♥ A K 10 8
♦ A Q
♣ 5

South	North
2♣	2♦
2♠	3♣
3♥	3♠
4NT	5♣
5NT	6♠

Opening Lead: ♠ 2

Trick 1 went 2, 7, 9, 10. Declarer managed to ruff a heart and later lost a diamond. Making six spades.

Could the defense have defeated the slam?

East threw away his chance to overruff dummy. He should note the doubleton heart in dummy, a suit South bid. What can he gain by covering the seven with the nine?

Playing random cards can be costly. Certainly playing the nine at Trick 1 can't help promote a trick for West.

175

DEAL 170. DUCK AND COUNTERDUCK;
THE FINAL STORY

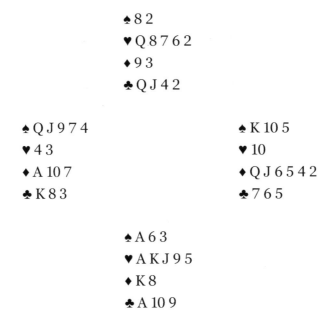

```
              ♠ 8 2
              ♥ Q 8 7 6 2
              ♦ 9 3
              ♣ Q J 4 2

♠ Q J 9 7 4                    ♠ K 10 5
♥ 4 3                          ♥ 10
♦ A 10 7                       ♦ Q J 6 5 4 2
♣ K 8 3                        ♣ 7 6 5

              ♠ A 6 3
              ♥ A K J 9 5
              ♦ K 8
              ♣ A 10 9
```

South	West	North	East
1♥	1♠	3♥*	3♠
4♥		All Pass	

•   Preemptive

Opening Lead: ♠ Queen

Declarer, having read Dr J's book and realizing the danger of East getting in and leading a diamond thru her king, correctly ducked the opening lead. She won West's ♠7 continuation and drew trumps.

After losing a club finesse to West, the safe hand, she was able to discard a diamond on a long club. Making four hearts, losing one spade, one diamond, and one club.

Well played or poorly defended?

Both. South's duck was fine. If East had read Dr J's book, at Trick 1 East will overtake the spade queen with the king. Failing to do so was fatal. If East overtakes, declarer has no winning option. If he ducks, East will switch to diamonds. If he wins, East has an entry with the spade 10 for the later diamond switch.

Special thanks to Mike Lawrence for this theme of punch and counter punch.

Printed in the United States
by Baker & Taylor Publisher Services